Your life can be easier...
more exciting...
more rewarding!

"Is there the faintest shadow of a reason why you should not be able to think as well in a perpendicular position before an audience as you can when sitting down? Surely, you know there is not. In fact, you ought to think better when facing a group. Their presence ought to stir and lift you. A great many speakers will tell you that the presence of an audience is a stimulus, an inspiration, that drives their brains to function more clearly, more keenly."

—Dale Carnegie

Here is a book for men and women who want to get ahead. As the author demonstrates on every page, the techniques that can put you over with an audience can help you in every phase of your life.

Books by Dale Carnegie

How to Develop Self-Confidence and Influence People by Public Speaking
How to Enjoy Your Life and Your Job (Revised Edition)
How to Stop Worrying and Start Living
How to Win Friends and Influence People (Revised Edition)
The Quick and Easy Way to Effective Speaking

By Dale Carnegie & Associates, Inc.

The Leader in You

Published by POCKET BOOKS

How to Develop Self-Confidence & Influence People by Public Speaking

Dale Carnegie

GALLERY BOOKS
New York London Toronto Sydney New Delhi

Gallery Books
An Imprint of Simon & Schuster, Inc.
1230 Avenue of the Americas
New York, NY 10020

This Gallery Books trade paperback edition July 2017

Manufactured in the United States of America

20 19 18 17 16 15 14 13

ISBN 978-1-5011-7198-7

Introduction

For many years, Dale Carnegie's name has been synonymous with winning friends and influencing people. *How to Win Friends and Influence People* is one of the best sellers of all time in nonfiction and has brought him international popularity. But *How to Win Friends and Influence People* was not the first book written by Dale Carnegie.

In 1926, Dale Carnegie wrote a book entitled *Public Speaking and Influencing Men in Business*. This was a textbook on public speaking, and, up to the present date, has been one of the official textbooks of the world-famous Dale Carnegie Course in Effective Speaking and Human Relations. It has also served as a textbook for Y.M.C.A. public-speaking classes. This book has sold 600,000 copies in the last ten years alone, and the total sale of the hard-cover edition is now over 1,000,000 copies. It has been published in some twenty languages and thousands of copies have been sold in these foreign editions. It has not, however, been a book of which the majority of the reading public has been aware.

Some time ago, the publisher, Association Press, approached me with the idea that this earliest of my late husband's books might have popular appeal if edited and published as a Pocket Book. They felt, as I do, that this book contained many valuable ideas for everyday living.

The Dale Carnegie Course has now spread its philosophy throughout the world and has reached a total of over 1,000,000 graduates. The course helps people to achieve a more courageous, happier and more fruitful life, by bringing out the latent qualities they possess.

This Pocket Book, *How to Develop Self-Confidence and Influence People by Public Speaking,* has been edited to appeal to the "reading" public. It contains many of the words of wisdom that have helped our students to achieve their goals. In re-reading the book carefully in the past few months, I realize how many wise rules it contains for overcoming fear and gaining self-confidence. Practical techniques and suggestions are added to those rules that will help everyone to meet people as individuals or as groups, and to talk with them effectively.

I do hope new readers will gain as much from this book as have the students of the Dale Carnegie Course in the past thirty years.

—DOROTHY CARNEGIE

Contents

How to Develop Self-Confidence and Influence People by Public Speaking

CHAPTER ONE

Developing Courage and Self-Confidence

More than five hundred thousand men and women, since 1912, have been members of public speaking courses using my methods. Many of them have written statements telling why they enrolled for this training and what they hoped to obtain from it. Naurally, the phraseology varied; but the central desire in these letters, the basic want in the vast majority, remained surprisingly the same: "When I am called upon to stand up and speak," person after person wrote, "I become so self-conscious, so frightened, that I can't think clearly, can't concentrate, can't remember what I had intended to say. I want to gain self-confidence, poise, and the ability to think on my feet. I want to get my thoughts together in logical order and I want to be able to say my say clearly and convincingly before a business or club group or audience." Thousands of their confessions sounded about like that.

To cite a concrete case: Years ago, a gentleman here called Mr. D. W. Ghent, joined my public speaking course in Philadelphia. Shortly after the opening session, he invited me to lunch with him in the Manufacturers' Club.

He was a man of middle age and had always led an active life; was head of his own manufacturing establishment, a leader in church work and civic activities. While we were having lunch that day, he leaned across the table and said: "I have been asked many times to talk before various gatherings, but I have never been able to do so. I get so fussed, my mind becomes an utter blank: so I have sidestepped it all my life. But I am chairman now of a board of college trustees. I must preside at their meetings. I simply have to do some talking. . . . Do you think it will be possible for me to learn to speak at this late date in my life?"

"Do I *think,* Mr. Ghent?" I replied. "It is *not* a question of my *thinking*. I *know you can,* and I *know you will* if you will only practice and follow the directions and instructions."

He wanted to believe that, but it seemed too rosy, too optimistic. "I am afraid you are just being kind," he answered, "that you are merely trying to encourage me."

After he had completed his training, we lost touch with each other for a while. Later, we met and lunched together again at the Manufacturers' Club. We sat in the same corner and occupied the same table that we had had on the first occasion. Reminding him of our former conversation, I asked him if I had been too sanguine then. He took a little red-backed notebook out of his pocket and showed me a list of talks and dates for which he was booked. "And the ability to make these," he confessed, "the pleasure I get in doing it, the additional service I can render to the community—these are among the most gratifying things in my life."

An important disarmament conference had been held in Washington shortly before that. When it was known that the British Prime Minister was planning to attend it, the Baptists of Philadelphia cabled, inviting him to speak at a great mass meeting to be held in their city. And Mr. Ghent informed me that he himself had been chosen, from among all the Baptists of that city, to introduce England's premier to the audience.

And this was the man who had sat at that same table less

than three years before and solemnly asked me if I thought he would ever be able to talk in public!

Was the rapidity with which he forged ahead in his speaking ability unusual? Not at all. There have been hundreds of similar cases. For example—to quote one more specific instance—years ago, a Brooklyn physician, whom we will call Dr. Curtis, spent the winter in Florida near the training grounds of the Giants. Being an enthusiastic baseball fan, he often went to see them practice. In time, he became quite friendly with the team, and was invited to attend a banquet given in their honor.

After the coffee and nuts were served, several prominent guests were called upon to "say a few words." Suddenly, with the abruptness and unexpectedness of an explosion, he heard the toastmaster remark: "We have a physician with us to-night, and I am going to ask Dr. Curtis to talk on a Baseball Player's Health."

Was he prepared? Of course. He had had the best preparation in the world: he had been studying hygiene and practicing medicine for almost a third of a century. He could have sat in his chair and talked about this subject all night to the man seated on his right or left. But to get up and say the same things to even a small audience—that was another matter. That was a paralyzing matter. His heart doubled its pace and skipped beats at the very contemplation of it. He had never made a public speech in his life, and every thought that he had had now took wings.

What was he to do? The audience was applauding. Everyone was looking at him. He shook his head. But that served only to heighten the applause, to increase the demand. The cries of "Dr. Curtis! Speech! Speech!" grew louder and more insistent.

He was in positive misery. He knew that if he got up he would fail, that he would be unable to utter half a dozen sentences. So he arose, and, without saying a word, turned his back on his friends and walked silently out of the room, a deeply embarrassed and humiliated man.

Small wonder that one of the first things he did after getting back to Brooklyn was to enroll in my course in Public

Speaking. He didn't propose to be put to the blush and be stricken dumb a second time.

He was the kind of student that delights an instructor: he was in dead earnest. He wanted to be able to talk, and there was no halfheartedness about his desire. He prepared his talks thoroughly, he practiced them with a will, and he never missed a single session of the course.

He did precisely what such a student always does: he progressed at a rate that surprised him, that surpassed his fondest hopes. After the first few sessions his nervousness subsided, his confidence mounted higher and higher. In two months he had become the star speaker of the group. He was soon accepting invitations to speak elsewhere; he now loved the feel and exhilaration of it, the distinction and the additional friends it brought him.

A member of the New York City Republican Campaign Committee, hearing one of his public addresses, invited Dr. Curtis to stump the city for his party. How surprised that politician would have been had he realized that only a year before, the speaker had gotten up and left a public banquet hall in shame and confusion because he was tongue-tied with audience-fear!

The gaining of self-confidence and courage, and the ability to think calmly and clearly while talking to a group is not one-tenth as difficult as most people imagine. It is not a gift bestowed by Providence on only a few rarely endowed individuals. It is like the ability to play golf. Anyone can develop his own latent capacity if he has sufficient desire to do so.

Is there the faintest shadow of a reason why you should not be able to think as well in a perpendicular position before an audience as you can when sitting down? Surely, you know there is not. In fact, you ought to think better when facing a group. Their presence ought to stir you and lift you. A great many speakers will tell you that the presence of an audience is a stimulus, an inspiration, that drives their brains to function more clearly, more keenly. At such times, thoughts, facts, ideas that they did not know they possessed, "drift smoking by," as Henry Ward Beecher said; and they have but to reach out and lay their hands hot upon them. That ought to be your experience. It probably will be if you practice and persevere.

Of this much, however, you may be absolutely sure: training and practice will wear away your audience-fright and give you self-confidence and an abiding courage.

Do not imagine that your case is unusually difficult. Even those who afterward became the most eloquent representatives of their generation were, at the outset of their careers, afflicted by this blinding fear and self-consciousness.

William Jennings Bryan, battle-marked veteran that he was, admitted that in his first attempts, his knees fairly smote together.

Mark Twain, the first time he stood up to lecture, felt as if his mouth were filled with cotton and his pulse were speeding for some prize cup.

Grant took Vicksburg and led to victory one of the greatest armies the world had ever seen up to that time; yet, when he attempted to speak in public, he admitted he had somehing very like locomotor ataxia.

The late Jean Jaurès, the most powerful political speaker that France produced during his generation, sat, for a year, tongue-tied in the Chamber of Deputies before he could summon up the courage to make his initial speech.

"The first time I attempted to make a public talk," confessed Lloyd George, "I tell you I was in a state of misery. It is no figure of speech, but literally true, that my tongue clove to the roof of my mouth; and, at first, I could hardly get out a word."

John Bright, the illustrious Englishman who, during the civil war, defended in England the cause of union and emancipation, made his maiden speech before a group of country folk gathered in a school building. He was so frightened on the way to the place, so fearful that he would fail, that he implored his companion to start applause to bolster him up whenever he showed signs of giving way to his nervousness.

Charles Stewart Parnell, the great Irish leader, at the outset of his speaking career, was so nervous, according to the testimony of his brother, that he frequently clenched his fists until his nails sank into his flesh and his palms bled.

Disraeli admitted that he would rather have led a cavalry charge than to have faced the House of Commons for the first time. His opening speech there was a ghastly failure. So was Sheridan's.

In fact, so many of the famous speakers of England have made poor showings at first that there is now a feeling in Parliament that it is rather an inauspicious omen for a young man's initial talk to be a decided success. So take heart.

After watching the careers and aiding somewhat in the development of so many speakers, the author is always glad when a student has, at the outset, a certain amount of flutter and nervous agitation.

There is a certain responsibility in making a talk, even if it is to only two dozen men or women in a business meeting—a certain strain, a certain shock, a certain excitement. The speaker ought to be keyed up like a thoroughbred straining at the bit. The immortal Cicero said, two thousand years ago, that all public speaking of real merit was characterized by nervousness.

Speakers often experience this same feeling even when they are talking over the radio. "Microphone fright," it is called. When Charlie Chaplin went on the air, he had his speech all written out. Surely he was used to audiences. He toured this country back in 1912 with a vaudeville sketch entitled "A Night in a Music Hall." Before that he was on the legitimate stage in England. Yet, when he went into the padded room and faced the microphone, he had a feeling in the stomach not unlike the sensation one gets when he crosses the Atlantic during a stormy February.

James Kirkwood, a famous motion picture actor and director, had a similar experience. He used to be a star on the speaking stage; but, when he came out of the sending room after addressing the invisible audience, he was mopping perspiration from his brow. "An opening night on Broadway," he confessed, "is nothing in comparison to that."

Some people, no matter how often they speak, always experience this self-consciousness just before they commence but, in a few sconds after they have gotten on their feet, it disappears.

Even Lincoln felt shy for the few opening moments. "At first he was very awkward," relates his law partner, Herndon, "and it seemed a real labor to adjust himself to his surroundings. He struggled for a time under a feeling of apparent diffidence and sensitiveness, and these only added to his awkwardness. I have often seen and sympathized with Mr. Lincoln during these moments. When he began speaking, his voice was shrill, piping, and unpleasant. His manner, his attitude, his dark, yellow face, wrinkled and dry, his oddity of pose, his diffident movements—everything seemed to be against him, but only for a short time." In a few moments he gained composure and warmth and earnestness, and his real speech began.

Your experience may be similar to his.

In order to get the most out of your efforts to become a good speaker in public, and to get it with rapidity and dispatch, four things are essential:

First: Start with a Strong and Persistent Desire

This is of far more importance than you probably realize. If an instructor could look into your mind and heart now and ascertain the depth of your desires, he could foretell, almost with certainty, the swiftness of the progress you will make. If your desire is pale and flabby, your achievements will also take on that hue and consistency. But, if you go after your subject with persistence, and with the energy of a bulldog after a cat, nothing underneath the Milky Way will defeat you.

Therefore, arouse your enthusiasm for this self-study. Enumerate its benefits. Think of what additional self-confidence and the ability to talk more convincingly in public will mean to you. Think of what it may mean and what it ought to mean, in dollars and cents. Think of what it may mean to you socially; of the friends it will bring, of the increase of your personal influence, of the leadership it will give you. And it will give you leadership more rapidly than almost any other activity you can think of or imagine.

"There is no other accomplishment," stated Chauncey M. Depew, "which any man can have that will so quickly make for him a career and secure recognition as the ability to speak acceptably."

Philip D. Armour, after he had amassed millions, said: "I would rather have been a great speaker than a great capitalist."

It is an attainment that almost every person of education longs for. After Andrew Carnegie's death there was found, among his papers, a plan for his life drawn up when he was thirty-three years of age. He then felt that in two more years he could so arrange his business as to have an annual income of fifty thousand; so he proposed to retire at thirty-five, go to Oxford and get a thorough education, and *"pay special attention to speaking in public."*

Think of the glow of satisfaction and pleasure that will accrue from the exercise of this new power. The author has traveled around over no small part of the world; and has had many and varied experiences; but for downright and lasting inward satisfaction, he knows of few things that will compare to standing before an audience and making men think your thoughts after you. It will give you a sense of strength, a feeling of power. It will appeal to your pride of personal accomplishment. It will set you off from and raise you above your fellow men. There is magic in it and a never-to-be-forgotten thrill. "Two minutes before I begin," a speaker confessed, "I would rather be whipped than start; but two minutes before I finish, I would rather be shot than stop."

In every effort, some men grow faint-hearted and fall by the wayside; so you should keep thinking of what this skill will mean to you until your desire is white hot. You should start this program with an enthusiasm that will carry you through triumphant to the end. Set aside one certain night of the week for the reading of these chapters. In short, make it as easy as possible to go ahead. Make it as difficult as possible to retreat.

When Julius Cæsar sailed over the channel from Gaul

and landed with his legions on what is now England, what did he do to insure the success of his arms? A very clever thing: he halted his soldiers on the chalk cliffs of Dover, and, looking down over the waves two hundred feet below, they saw red tongues of fire consume every ship in which they had crossed. In the enemy's country, with the last link with the Continent gone, the last means of retreating burned, there was but one thing left for them to do: to advance, to conquer. That is precisely what they did.

Such was the spirit of the immortal Cæsar. Why not make it yours, too, in this war to exterminate any foolish fear of audiences?

Second: Know Thoroughly What You Are Going to Talk About

Unless a person has thought out and planned his talk and knows what he is going to say, he can't feel very comfortable when he faces his auditors. He is like the blind leading the blind. Under such circumstances, your speaker ought to be self-conscious, ought to feel repentant, ought to be ashamed of his negligence.

"I was elected to the Legislature in the fall of 1881," Teddy Roosevelt wrote in his *Autobiography*, "and found myself the youngest man in that body. Like all young men and inexperienced members, I had considerable difficulty in teaching myself to speak. I profited much by the advice of a hard-headed old countryman—who was unconsciously paraphrasing the Duke of Wellington, who was himself doubtless paraphrasing somebody else. The advice ran: 'Don't speak until you are sure you have something to say, and know just what it is; then say it, and sit down.' "

This "hard-headed old countryman" ought to have told Roosevelt of another aid in overcoming nervousness. He ought to have added: "It will help you to throw off embarrassment if you can find something to do before an audience—if you can exhibit something, write a word on the blackboard, or point out a spot on the map, or move a table, or throw open a window, or shift some books and papers—any physical action with a purpose behind it may help you to feel more at home."

True, it is not always easy to find an excuse for doing such things; but there is the suggestion. Use it if you can; but use it the first few times only. A baby does not cling to chairs after it once learns to walk.

Third: Act Confident

One of the most famous psychologists that America has produced, Professor William James, wrote as follows:

> Action seems to follow feeling, but really action and feeling go together; and by regulating the action, which is under the more direct control of the will, we can indirectly regulate the feeling, which is not.
>
> Thus the sovereign voluntary path to cheerfulness, if our spontaneous cheerfulness be lost, is to sit up cheerfully and to act and speak as if cheerfulness were already there. If such conduct does not make you feel cheerful, nothing else on that occasion can.
>
> So, to feel brave, act as if we were brave, use all of our will to that end, and a courage fit will very likely replace the fit of fear.

Apply Professor James' advice. To develop courage when you are facing an audience, act as if you already had it. Of course, unless you are prepared, all the acting in the world will avail but little. But granted that you know what you are going to talk about, step out briskly and take a deep breath. In fact, breathe deeply for thirty seconds before you ever face your audience. The increased supply of oxygen will buoy you up and give you courage. The great tenor, Jean de Reszke, used to say that when you had your breath so you "could sit on it" nervousness vanished.

In every age, in every clime, men have always admired courage; so, no matter how your heart may be pounding inside, stride forth bravely, stop, stand still and act as if you loved it.

Draw yourself up to your full height, look your audience straight in the eyes, and begin to talk as confidently as if every one of them owed you money. Imagine that they do. Imagine that they have assembled there to beg you for an extension of credit. The psychological effect on you will be beneficial.

Do not nervously button and unbutton your coat, play with your beads, or fumble with your hands. If you must make nervous movements, place your hands behind your back and twist your fingers there where no one can see the performance—or wiggle your toes.

As a general rule, it is bad for a speaker to hide behind furniture; but it may give you a little courage the first few times to stand behind a table or chair and to grip them tightly—or hold a coin firmly in the palm of your hand.

How did Teddy Roosevelt develop his characteristic courage and self-reliance? Was he endowed by nature with a venturesome and daring spirit? Not at all. "Having been a rather sickly and awkward boy," he confesses in his *Autobiography,* "I was, as a young man, at first both nervous and distrustful of my own prowess. I had to train myself painfully and laboriously not merely as regards my body but as regards my soul and spirit."

Fortunately, he has told us how he achieved the transformation: "When a boy," he writes, "I read a passage in one of Marryat's books which always impressed me. In this passage the captain of some small British man-of-war is explaining to the hero how to acquire the quality of fearlessness. He says that at the outset almost every man is frightened when he goes into action, but that the course to follow is for the man to keep such a grip on himself that he can act just as if he were not frightened. After this is kept up long enough, it changes from pretense to reality, and the man does in very fact become fearless by sheer dint of practicing fearlessness when he does not feel it. (I am using my own language, not Marryat's.)

"This was the theory upon which I went. There were all kinds of things of which I was afraid at first, ranging from grizzly bears to 'mean' horses and gun-fighters; but by acting as if I was not afraid I gradually ceased to be afraid. Most men can have the same experience if they choose."

You can have that very experience, too, if you wish. "In war," said Marshal Foch, "the best defensive is an offensive." So take the offensive against your fears. Go out to meet them, battle them, conquer them by sheer boldness at every opportunity.

Have a message, and then think of yourself as a Western Union boy instructed to deliver it. We pay slight attention to the boy. It is the telegram that we want. The message—that is the thing. Keep your mind on it. Keep your heart in it. Know it like the back of your hand. Believe it feelingly. Then talk as if you were determined to say it. Do that, and the chances are ten to one that you will soon be master of the occasion and master of yourself.

Fourth: Practice! Practice! Practice!

The last point we have to make here is emphatically the most important. Even though you forget everything you have read so far, do remember this: the first way, the last way, the never-failing way to develop self-confidence in speaking is—to speak. Really the whole matter finally simmers down to but one essential; practice, practice, practice. That is the *sine qua non* of it all, "the without which not."

"Any beginner," warned Roosevelt, "is apt to have 'buck fever.' 'Buck fever' means a state of intense nervous excitement which may be entirely divorced from timidity. It may affect a man the first time he has to speak to a large audience just as it may affect him the first time he sees a buck or goes into battle. What such a man needs is not courage, but nerve control, coolheadedness. *This he can get only by actual practice. He must, by custom and repeated exercise of self-mastery, get his nerves thoroughly under control. This is largely a matter of habit; in the sense of repeated effort and repeated exercise of will power. If the man has the right stuff in him, he will grow stronger and stronger with each exercise of it."*

You want to get rid of your audience fear? Let us see what causes it.

"Fear is begotten of ignorance and uncertainty," says Professor Robinson in *The Mind in the Making.* To put it another way: it is the result of a lack of confidence.

And what causes that? It is the result of not knowing what you can really do. And not knowing what you can do is caused by a lack of experience. When you get a record of successful experience behind you, your fears will vanish; they will melt like night mists under the glare of a July sun.

One thing is certain: the accepted way to learn to swim is to plunge into the water. You have been reading this book long enough. Why not toss it aside now, and get busy with the real work in hand.

Choose your subject, preferably one on which you have some knowledge, and construct a three-minute talk. Practice the talk by yourself a number of times. Then give it, if possible, to the group for whom it is intended, or before a group of friends, putting into the effort all your force and power.

Summary

1. A few thousand students have written the author stating why they wanted training in public speaking and what they hoped to obtain from it. The prime reason that almost all of them gave was this: they wanted to conquer their nervousness, to be able to think on their feet, and to speak with self-confidence and ease before a group of any size.

2. The ability to do this is not difficult to acquire. It is not a gift bestowed by Providence on only a few rarely endowed individuals. It is like the ability to play golf: any man or woman—every person—can develop his own latent capacity if he has sufficient desire to do so.

3. Many experienced speakers can think better and talk better when facing a group than they can in conversation with an individual. The presence of the larger number proves to be a stimulus, an inspiration. If you faithfully follow the suggestions in this book, the time may come when that will be your experience, too; and you will look forward with positive pleasure to making an address.

4. Do not imagine that your case is unusual. Many men who afterward became famous speakers were, at the outset of their careers, beset with self-consciousness and almost paralyzed with audience fright. This was the experience of Bryan, Jean Jaurès, Lloyd George, Charles Stewart Parnell, John Bright, Disraeli, Sheridan and a host of others.

5. No matter how often you speak, you may always experience this self-consciousness just before you begin; but, in a few seconds after you have gotten on your feet, it will vanish completely.

6. In order to get the most out of this book and to get it with rapidity and dispatch, do these four things:

a. Start with a strong and persistent desire. Enumerate the benefits this effort to train yourself will bring you. Arouse your enthusiasm for it. Think what it can mean to you financially, socially and in terms of increased influence and leadership. Remember that upon the depth of your desire will depend the swiftness of your progress.

b. Prepare. You can't feel confident unless you know what you are going to say.

c. Act confident. "To feel brave," advises Professor William James, "act as if we were brave, use all of our will to that end, and a courage fit will very likely replace the fit of fear." Teddy Roosevelt confessed that he conquered his fear of grizzly bears, mean horses, and gunfighters by that method. You can conquer your fear of audiences by taking advantage of this psychological fact.

d. Practice. This is the most important point of all. Fear is the result of a lack of confidence; and a lack of confidence is the result of not knowing what you can do; and that is caused by a lack of experience. So get a record of successful experience behind you, and your fears will vanish.

CHAPTER TWO

Self-Confidence Through Preparation

It has been the author's professional duty as well as his pleasure to listen to and criticize approximately six thousand speeches a year each season since 1912. These were made, not by college students, but by mature business and professional men. If that experience has engraved on his mind any one thing more deeply than another, surely it is this: the urgent necessity of preparing a talk before one starts to make it and of having something clear and definite to say, something that has impressed one, something that won't stay unsaid. Aren't you unconsciously drawn to the speaker who, you feel, has a real message in his head and heart that he zealously desires to communicate to your head and heart? That is half the secret of speaking.

When a speaker is in that kind of mental and emotional state he will discover a significant fact: namely, that his talk will almost make itself. Its yoke will be easy, its burden will be light. A well-prepared speech is already nine-tenths delivered.

The primary reason why most people want this training, as was recorded in Chapter I, is to acquire confidence and courage and self-reliance. And the one fatal mistake many make is neglecting to prepare their talks. How can they even hope to subdue the cohorts of fear, the cavalry of nervousness, when they go into the battle with wet powder and blank shells, or with no ammunition at all? Under the circumstances, small wonder that they are not exactly at home before an audience. "I believe," said Lincoln in the White House, "that I shall never be old enough to speak without embarrassment when I have nothing to say."

If you want confidence, why not do the things necessary to bring it about? "Perfect love," wrote the Apostle John, "casteth out fear." So does perfect preparation. Webster said he would as soon think of appearing before an audience half-clothed as half-prepared.

Why don't we prepare our talks more carefully? Why? Some don't clearly understand what preparation is nor how to go about it wisely; others plead a lack of time. So we shall discuss these problems rather fully in this chapter.

The Right Way to Prepare

What is preparation? Reading a book? That is one kind, but not the best. Reading may help; but if one attempts to lift a lot of "canned" thoughts out of a book and to give them out immediately as his own, the whole performance will be lacking in something. The audience may not know precisely what is lacking, but they will not warm to the speaker.

To illustrate: some time ago, the writer conducted a course in public speaking for the senior officers of New York City banks. Naturally, the members of such a group, having many demands upon their time, frequently found it difficult to prepare adequately, or to do what they conceived of as preparing. All their lives they had been thinking their own individual thoughts, nurturing their own personal convictions, seeing things from their own distinctive angles, living their own original experiences. So, in that fashion, they had spent forty years storing up material for speeches. But it was hard for some of them to realize that.

They could not see the forest for "the murmuring pines and the hemlocks."

This group met Friday evenings from five to seven. One Friday, a certain gentleman connected with an uptown bank —for our purposes we shall designate him as Mr. Jackson —found four-thirty had arrived, and, what was he to talk about? He walked out of his office, bought a copy of *Forbes' Magazine* at a news stand and, in the subway coming down to the Federal Reserve Bank where the class met, he read an article entitled, "You Have Only Ten Years to Succeed." He read it, not because he was interested in the article especially; but because he must speak on something, on anything, to fill his quota of time.

An hour later, he stood up and attempted to talk convincingly and interestingly on the contents of this article.

What was the result, the inevitable result?

He had not digested, had not assimilated what he was trying to say. "Trying to say"—that expresses it precisely. He was *trying*. There was no real message in him seeking for an outlet; and his whole manner and tone revealed it unmistakably. How could he expect the audience to be any more impressed than he himself was? He kept referring to the article, saying the author said so and so. There was a surfeit of *Forbes' Magazine* in it: but regrettably little of Mr. Jackson.

So the writer addressed him somewhat in this fashion: "Mr. Jackson, we are not interested in this shadowy personality who wrote that article. He is not here. We can't see him. But we are interested in you and your ideas. Tell us what you think, personally, not what somebody else said. Put more of Mr. Jackson in this. Why not take this same subject for next week? Why not read this article again, and ask yourself whether you agree with the author or not? If you do, think out his suggestions and illustrate them with observations from your own experience. If you don't agree with him, say so and tell us why. Let this article be merely the starting point from which you launch your own speech."

Mr. Jackson accepted the suggestion, reread the article and concluded that he did not agree with the author at all. He did not sit down in the subway and try to prepare this next speech to order. He let it grow. It was a child of his own brain; and it developed and expanded and took on stature just as his physical children had done. And like his daughters, this other child grew day and night when he was least conscious of it. One thought was suggested to him while reading some item in the newspaper; another illustration swam into his mind unexpectedly when he was discussing the subject with a friend. The thing deepened and heightened, lengthened and thickened as he thought over it during the odd moments of the week.

The next time Mr. Jackson spoke on this subject, he had something that was his, ore that he dug out of his own mine, currency coined in his own mint. And he spoke all the better because he was disagreeing with the author of the article. There is no spur to rouse one like a little opposition.

What an incredible contrast between these two speeches by the same man, in the same fortnight, on the same subject. What a colossal difference the right kind of preparation makes!

Let us cite another illustration of how to do it and how not to do it. A gentleman, whom we shall call Mr. Flynn, was a student of public speaking in Washington, D.C. One afternoon he devoted his talk to eulogizing the capital city of the nation. He had hastily and superficially gleaned his facts from a booster booklet issued by a newspaper. They sounded like it—dry, disconnected, undigested. He had not thought over his subject adequately. It had not elicited his enthusiasm. He did not feel what he was saying deeply enough to make it worth while expressing. The whole affair was flat and flavorless and unprofitable.

A Speech That Could Not Fail

A fortnight later, something happened that touched Mr. Flynn to the core: a thief stole his car out of a public garage. He rushed to the police and offered rewards, but it was all in vain. The police admitted that it was well nigh impossible for them to cope with the crime situation; yet, only a week previously, they had found time to walk about the street, chalk in hand, and fine Mr. Flynn because he had parked his car fifteen minutes overtime. These "chalk cops," who were so busy that they could not catch criminals, aroused his ire. He was indignant. He had something now to say, not something that he had gotten out of a booklet issued by the newspaper, but something that was leaping hot out of his own life and experience. Here was something that was part and parcel of the real man—something that had aroused his feelings and convictions. In his speech eulogizing the city of Washington, he had laboriously pulled out sentence by sentence; but now he had but to stand on his feet and open his mouth, and his condemnation of the police welled up and boiled forth like Vesuvius in action. A speech like that is almost foolproof. It can hardly fail. It was experience plus reflection.

What Preparation Really Is

Does the preparation of a speech mean the getting together of some faultless phrases written down or memorized? No. Does it mean the assembling of a few casual thoughts that really convey very little to you personally? Not at all. It means the assembling of *your* thoughts, *your* ideas, *your* convictions, *your* urges. And you have such thoughts, such urges. You have them every day of your waking life. They even swarm through your dreams. Your whole existence has been filled with feelings and experiences. These things are lying deep in your subconscious mind as thick as pebbles on the seashore. Preparation means thinking, brooding, recalling, selecting the ones that appeal to you most, polishing them, working them into a pattern, a mosaic of your own. That doesn't sound like such a difficult program, does it? It isn't. Just requires a little concentration and thinking to a purpose.

How did Dwight L. Moody prepare those addresses of his which made spiritual history? "I have no secret," he replied in answer to that question.

When I choose a subject, I write the name of it on the

outside of a large envelope. I have many such envelopes. If, when I am reading, I meet a good thing on any subject I am to speak on, I slip it into the right envelope, and let it lie there. I always carry a notebook, and if I hear anything in a sermon that will throw light on that subject, I put it down, and slip it into the envelope. Perhaps I let it lie there for a year or more. When I want a new sermon, I take everything that has been accumulating. Between what I find there and the results of my own study, I have material enough. Then, all the time I am going over my sermons, taking out a little here, adding a little there. In that way they never get old.

The Sage Advice of Dean Brown of Yale

When the Yale Divinity School celebrated the one hundredth anniversary of its founding, the Dean, Dr. Charles Reynolds Brown, delivered a series of lectures on the Art of Preaching. These were published in book form under that name by the Macmillan Company, New York. Dr. Brown had been preparing addresses himself weekly for a third of a century, and also training others to prepare and deliver; so he was in a position to dispense some sage advice on the subject, advice that will hold good regardless of whether the speaker is a man of the cloth preparing a discourse on the Ninety-first Psalm, or a shoe manufacturer preparing a speech on Labor Unions. So I am taking the liberty of quoting Dr. Brown here:

> Brood over your text and your topic. Brood over them until they become mellow and responsive. You will hatch out of them a whole flock of promising ideas as you cause the tiny germs of life there contained to expand and develop. . . .
>
> It will be all the better if this process can go on for a long time and not be postponed until Saturday forenoon when you are actually making your final preparation for next Sunday. If a minister can hold a certain truth in his mind for a month, for six months perhaps, for a year it

may be, before he preaches on it he will find new ideas perpetually sprouting out of it, until it shows an abundant growth. He may meditate on it as he walks the streets, or as he spends some hours on a train, when his eyes are too tired to read.

He may indeed brood upon it in the night-time. It is better for the minister not to take his church or his sermon to bed with him habitually—a pulpit is a splendid thing to preach from, but it is not a good bed-fellow. Yet, for all that, I have sometimes gotten out of bed in the middle of the night to put down the thoughts which came to me, for fear I might forget them before morning. . . .

When you are actually engaged in assembling the material for a particular sermon, write down everything that comes to you bearing upon that text and topic. Write down what you saw in the text when you first chose it. Write down all the associated ideas which now occur to you. . . .

Put all these ideas of yours down in writing, just a few words, enough to fix the idea, and keep your mind reaching for more all the time as if it were never to see another book as long as it lived. This is the way to train the mind in productiveness. You will by this method keep your own mental processes fresh, original, creative. . . .

Put down all of those ideas which you have brought to the birth yourself, unaided. They are more precious for your mental unfolding than rubies and diamonds and much fine gold. Put them down, preferably on scraps of paper, backs of old letters, fragments of envelopes, waste paper, anything which comes to your hand. This is much better every way than to use nice, long, clean sheets of foolscap. It is not a mere matter of economy—you will find it easier to arrange and organize those loose bits when you come to set your material in order.

Keep on putting down all the ideas which come to your mind, thinking hard all the while. You need not hurry this process. It is one of the most important mental transactions in which you will be privileged to engage. It is this method which causes the mind to grow in real productive power. . . .

You will find that the sermons you enjoy preaching the most and the ones which actually accomplish the most good in the lives of your people will be those sermons which you take most largely out of your own interiors. They are bone of your bone, flesh of your flesh, the children of your own mental labor, the output of your own creative energy. The sermons which are garbled and compiled will always have a kind of second-hand, warmed-over flavor about them. The sermons which live and move and enter into the temple, walking and leaping and praising God, the sermons which enter into the hearts of men causing them to mount up with wings like eagles and to walk in the way of duty and not faint—these real sermons are the ones which are actually born from the vital energies of the man who utters them.

How Lincoln Prepared His Speeches

How did Lincoln prepare his speeches? Fortunately, we know the facts; and, as you read here of his method, you will observe that Dean Brown, in his lecture, commended several of the procedures that Lincoln had employed three-quarters of a century previously. One of Lincoln's most famous addresses was that in which he declared with prophetic vision: " 'A house divided against itself cannot stand.' I believe this government cannot endure, permanently, half slave and half free." This speech was thought out as he went about his usual work, as he ate his meals, as he walked the street, as he sat in his barn milking his cow, as he made his daily trip to the butcher shop and grocery, an old gray shawl over his shoulders, his market basket over his arm, his little son at his side, chattering and questioning, growing peeved, and jerking at the long bony fingers in a vain effort to make his father talk to him. But Lincoln stalked on, absorbed in his own reflections, thinking of his speech, apparently unconscious of the boy's existence.

From time to time during this brooding and hatching process, he jotted down notes, fragments, sentences here and there on stray envelopes, scraps of paper, bits torn from paper sacks—anything that was near. These he stowed away in the top of his hat and carried them there until he was ready to sit down and arrange them in order, and to write and revise the whole thing, and to shape it up for delivery and publication.

In the joint debates of 1858, Senator Douglas delivered the same speech wherever he went; but Lincoln kept studying and contemplating and reflecting until he found it easier, he said, to make a new speech each day than to repeat an old one. The subject was forever widening and enlarging in his mind.

A short time before he moved into the White House, he took a copy of the Constitution and three speeches, and with only these for reference, he locked himself in a dingy, dusty back room over a store in Springfield; and there, away from all intrusion and interruption, he wrote out his inaugural address.

How did Lincoln prepare his Gettysburg address? Unfortunately, false reports have been circulated about it. The true story, however, is fascinating. Let us have it:

When the commission in charge of the Gettysburg cemetery decided to arrange for a formal dedication, they invited Edward Everett to deliver the speech. He had been a Boston minister, president of Harvard, governor of Massachusetts, United States senator, minister to England, secretary of state, and was generally considered to be America's most capable speaker. The date first set for the dedication ceremonies was October 23, 1863. Mr. Everett very wisely declared that it would be impossible for him to prepare adequately on such short notice. So the dedication was postponed until November 19, nearly a month, to give him time to prepare. The last three days of that period he spent in Gettysburg, going over the battlefield, familiarizing himself with all that had taken place there. That period of brooding and thinking was most excellent preparation. It made the battle real to him.

Invitations to be present were despatched to all the members of Congress, to the President and his cabinet. Most of these declined; the committee was surprised when Lincoln agreed to come. Should they ask him to speak? They had not intended to do so. Objections were raised. He would not have time to prepare. Besides, even if he did have time, had he the ability? True, he could handle himself well in a debate on slavery or in a Cooper Union address; but no one had ever heard him deliver a dedicatory address. This was a grave and solemn occasion. They ought not to take any chances. Should they ask him to speak? They wondered, wondered. . . . But they would have wondered a thousand times more had they been able to look into the future and to see that this man, whose ability they were questioning, was to deliver on that occasion what is very generally accepted now as one of the most enduring addresses ever delivered by the lips of mortal man.

Finally, a fortnight before the event, they sent Lincoln a belated invitation to make "a few appropriate remarks." Yes, that is the way they worded it: "a few appropriate remarks." Think of writing that to the President of the United States!

Lincoln immediately set about preparing. He wrote to Edward Everett, secured a copy of the address that that classic scholar was to deliver, and, a day or two later, going to a photographer's gallery to pose for his photograph, took Everett's manuscript with him and read it during the spare time that he had at the studio. He thought over his talk for days, thought over it while walking back and forth between the White House and the war office, thought over it while stretched out on a leather couch in the war office waiting for the late telegraphic reports. He wrote a rough draft of it on a piece of foolscap paper, and carried it about in the top of his tall silk hat. Ceaselessly he was brooding over it, ceaselessly it was taking shape. The Sunday before it was delivered he said to Noah Brooks: "It is not exactly written. It is not finished anyway. I have written it over two or three times, and I shall have to give it another lick before I am satisfied."

He arrived in Gettysburg the night before the dedication. The little town was filled to overflowing. Its usual population of thirteen hundred had been suddenly swelled to fifteen thousand. The sidewalks became clogged, impassable; men and women took to the dirt streets. Half a dozen bands were playing; crowds were singing "John Brown's Body." People fore-gathered before the home of Mr. Wills where Lincoln was being entertained. They serenaded him; they demanded a speech. Lincoln responded with a few words which conveyed with more clearness than tact, perhaps, that he was unwilling to speak until the morrow. The facts are that he was spending the latter part of that evening giving his speech "another lick." He even went to an adjoining house where Secretary Seward was staying and read the speech aloud to him for his criticism. After breakfast the next morning, he continued "to give it another lick," working on it until a rap came at the door informing him that it was time for him to take his place in the procession. "Colonel Carr, who rode just behind the President, stated that when the procession started, the President sat erect on his horse, and looked the part of the commander-in-chief of the army; but, as the procession moved on, his body leaned forward, his arms hung limp, and his head was bowed. He seemed absorbed in thought."

We can only guess that even then he was going over his little speech of ten immortal sentences, giving it "another lick."

Some of Lincoln's speeches, in which he had only a superficial interest, were unquestioned failures; but he was possessed of extraordinary power when he spoke of slavery and the union. Why? Because he thought ceaselessly on these problems and felt deeply. A companion who shared a room with him one night in an Illinois tavern awoke next morning at daylight to find Lincoln sitting up in bed, staring at the wall, and his first words were: "This government cannot endure permanently, half slave and half free."

How did Christ prepare his addresses? He withdrew from the crowd. He thought. He brooded. He pondered. He went out alone into the wilderness and meditated and fasted for forty days and forty nights. "From that time on," records Saint Matthew, "Jesus began to preach." Shortly after that, he delivered one of the world's most celebrated speeches: the Sermon on the Mount.

"That is all very interesting," you may protest; "but I have no desire to become an immortal orator. I merely want to make a few simple talks occasionally."

True, and we realize your wants fully. This book is for the specific purpose of helping you and others like you to do just that. But, unpretending as the talks of yours may prove to be, you can profit by and utilize in some measure the methods of the famous speakers of the past.

How to Prepare Your Talk

What topics ought you to speak on for practice? Anything that interests you. Don't make the almost universal mistake of trying to cover too much ground in a brief talk. Just take one or two angles of a subject and attempt to cover them adequately. You will be fortunate if you can do that in a short speech.

Determine your subject in advance, so that you will have time to think it over in odd moments. Think over it for seven days; dream over it for seven nights. Think of it the last thing when you retire. Think of it the next morning while you are shaving, while you are bathing, while you are riding down town, while you are waiting for elevators, for lunch, for appointments, while you are ironing or cooking dinner. Discuss it with your friends. Make it a topic of conversation.

Ask yourself all possible questions concerning it. If, for example, you are to speak on divorce, ask yourself what causes divorce, what are the effects economically, socially. How can the evil be remedied? Should we have uniform divorce laws? Why? Or should we have any divorce laws? Should divorce be made impossible? More difficult? Easier?

Suppose you were going to talk on why you are studying speech. You ought then to ask yourself such questions as these: What are my troubles? What do I hope to get out of this? Have I ever made a public talk? If so, when? Where? What happened? Why do I think this training is valuable for a business man? Do I know men and women who are forging ahead commercially or in politics largely because of their self-confidence, their presence, their ability to talk convincingly? Do I know others who will probably never achieve a gratifying measure of success because they lack these positive assets? Be specific. Tell the stories of these people without mentioning their names.

If you stand up and think clearly and keep going for two or three minutes, that is all that can be expected of you during your first few talks. A topic such as why you are studying public speaking, is very easy; that is obvious. If you will spend a little time selecting and arranging your material on that topic, you will be almost sure to remember it, for you will be speaking of your own observations, your own desires, your own experiences.

On the other hand, let us suppose that you have decided to speak on your business or profession. How shall you set about preparing such a talk? You already have a wealth of material on that subjcct. Your problem, then, will be to select and arrange it. Do not attempt to tell us all about it in three minutes. It can't be done. The attempt will be too sketchy, too fragmentary. Take one and only one phase of your topic: expand and enlarge that. For example, why not tell how you came to be in your particular business or profession? Was it a result of accident or choice? Relate your early struggles, your defeats, your hopes, your triumphs. Give a human interest narrative, a real life picture based on firsthand experiences. The truthful, inside story of almost anyone's life—if told modestly and without offending egotism—is most entertaining. It is almost sure-fire speech material.

Or take another angle of your business: what are its troubles? What advice would you give to a young person entering it?

Or tell about the people with whom you come in contact —the honest and dishonest ones. Tell of your problems. What has your work taught you about the most interesting topic in the world: human nature? If you speak about the technical side of your job, about things, your talk may very easily prove uninteresting to others. But people, personalities—one can hardly go wrong with that kind of material.

Above all else, don't make your talk an abstract preachment. That will bore. Make your talk a regular layer cake of illustrations and general statements. Think of concrete cases you have observed, and of the fundamental truths which you believe those specific instances illustrate. You will also discover that these concrete cases are far easier to remember than abstractions; are far easier to talk about. They will also aid and brighten your delivery.

Here is the way a very interesting writer does it. This is an excerpt from an article by B. A. Forbes on the necessity of executives' delegating responsibilities to their associates. Note the illustrations—the gossip about people.

> Many of our present-day gigantic enterprises were at one time one-man affairs. But most of them have outgrown this status. The reason is that, while every great organization is 'the lengthened shadow of one man,' business and industry are now conducted on such a colossal scale that of necessity even the ablest giant must gather about him brainy associates to help in handling all the reins.
>
> Woolworth once told me that his was essentially a one-man business for years. Then he ruined his health, and it was while he lay week after week in the hospital that he awakened to the fact that if his business was to expand as he hoped, he would have to share the managerial responsibilities.
>
> Bethlehem Steel for a number of years was distinctly of the one-man type. Charles M. Schwab was the whole works. By and by Eugene G. Grace grew in stature and developed into an abler steel man than Schwab, according to the repeated declarations of the latter.
>
> Eastman Kodak in its earlier stages consisted mainly of George Eastman, but he was wise enough to create an efficient organization long ago. All the greatest Chicago packing houses underwent a similar experience during the time of their founders. Standard Oil, contrary to the

popular notion, never was a one-man organization after it grew to large dimensions.

J. P. Morgan, although a towering giant, was an ardent believer in choosing the most capable partners and sharing the burdens with them.

There are still ambitious business leaders who would like to run their business on the one-man principle, but, willy-nilly, they are forced by the very magnitude of modern operations to delegate responsibilities to others.

Some men, in speaking of their businesses, commit the unforgivable error of talking only of the features that interest them. Shouldn't the speaker try to ascertain what will entertain not himself but his hearers? Shouldn't he try to appeal to their selfish interests? If, for example, he sells fire insurance, shouldn't he tell them how to prevent fires on their own property? If he is a banker, shouldn't he give them advice on finance or investments? If the speaker is a national leader of a women's organization, shouldn't she tell her local audience of the ways they are part of a national movement by citing specific examples from their local program?

While preparing, study your audience. Think of their wants, their wishes. That is sometimes half the battle.

In preparing some topics, it is very advisable to do some reading, to discover what others have thought, what others have said on the same subject. But don't read until you have first thought yourself dry. That is important—very. Then go to the public library and lay your needs before the librarian. Tell her you are preparing a speech on such and such a topic. Ask her frankly for help. If you are not in the habit of doing research work, you will probably be surprised at the aids she can put at your disposal; perhaps a special volume on your very topic, outlines and briefs for debate, giving the principal arguments on both sides of the public questions of the day; the Reader's Guide to Periodical Literature listing the magazine articles that have appeared on various topics since the beginning of the century; Information Please Almanac, the World Almanac, the Encyclopedias, and dozens of reference books. They are tools in your workshop. Use them.

The Secret of Reserve Power

Luther Burbank said, shortly before his death: "I have often produced a million plant specimens to find but one or two superlatively good ones, and have then destroyed all the inferior specimens." A speech ought to be prepared somewhat in that lavish and discriminating spirit. Assemble a hundred thoughts, and discard ninety.

Collect more material, more information, than there is any possibility of employing. Get it for the additional confidence it will give you, for the sureness of touch. Get it for the effect it will have on your mind and heart and whole manner of speaking. This is a basic, important factor of preparation; yet it is constantly ignored by speakers, both in public and in private.

"I have drilled hundreds of salesmen and saleswomen, canvassers, and demonstrators," says Arthur Dunn, "and the principal weakness which I have discovered in most of them has been their failure to realize the importance of knowing everything possible about their products and getting such knowledge before they start to sell.

"Many salesmen have come to my office and after getting a description of the article and a line of sales talk have been eager to get right out and try to sell. Many of these salesmen have not lasted a week and a large number have not lasted forty-eight hours. In educating and drilling canvassers and salesmen in the sale of a food specialty, I have endeavored to make food experts of them. I have compelled them to study food charts issued by the U. S. Department of Agriculture, which show in food the amount of water, the amount of protein, the amount of carbohydrates, the amount of fat, and ash. I have had them study the elements which make up the products which they are to sell. I have had them go to school for several days and then pass examinations. I have had them sell the product to other salesmen. I have offered prizes for the best sales talks.

"I have often found salesmen who get impatient at the preliminary time required for the study of their articles. They have said, 'I will never have time to tell all of this to a retail grocer. He is too busy. If I talk protein and carbohydrates, he won't listen and, if he does listen, he won't know what I am talking about.' My reply has been, 'You don't get all this knowledge for the benefit of your customer, but for the benefit of yourself. If you know your product from A to Z you will have a feeling about it that is difficult to describe. You will be so positively charged, so fortified, so strengthened in your own mental attitude that you will be both irresistible and unconquerable.' "

Miss Ida M. Tarbell, the well-known historian of the Standard Oil Company, told the writer that years ago, when she was in Paris, Mr. S. S. McClure, the founder of *McClure's Magazine*, cabled her to write a short article about the Atlantic Cable. She went to London, interviewed the European manager of the principal cable, and obtained sufficient data for her assignment. But she did not stop there. She wanted a reserve supply of facts; so she studied all manner of cables on display in the British Museum; she read books on the history of the cable and even went to manufacturing concerns on the edge of London and saw cables in the process of construction.

Why did she collect ten times as much information as she could possibly use? She did it because she felt it would give her reserve power; because she realized that the things she knew and did not express would lend force and color to the little she did express.

Edwin James Cattell has spoken to approximately thirty million people; yet he confided to me that if he did not, on the way home, kick himself for the good things he had left out of his talk he felt that the performance must have been a failure. Why? Because he knew from long experience that the talks of distinct merit are those in which there abounds a reserve of material, a plethora, a profusion of it—far more than the speaker has time to use.

Summary

1. When a speaker has a real message in his head and heart—an inner urge to speak, he is almost sure to do himself credit. A well-prepared speech is already nine-tenths delivered.

2. What is preparation? The setting down of some mechanical sentences on paper? The memorizing of phrases? Not at all. Real preparation consists in digging something out of yourself, in assembling and arranging *your own* thoughts, in cherishing and nurturing *your own* convictions. (Illustrations: Mr. Jackson of New York failed when he attempted merely to reiterate another man's thoughts he had culled from an article in *Forbes' Magazine.* He succeeded when he used that article merely as a starting point for his own speech—when he thought out *his own* ideas, developed *his own* illustrations.)

3. Do not sit down and try to manufacture a speech in thirty minutes. A speech can't be cooked to order like a steak. A speech must *grow.* Select your topic early in the week, think over it during odd moments, brood over it, sleep over it, dream over it. Discuss it with friends. Make it a topic of conversation. Ask yourself all possible questions concerning it. Put down on pieces of paper all thoughts and illustrations that come to you and keep reaching out for more. Ideas, suggestions, illustrations will come drifting to you at sundry times—when you are bathing, when you are driving downtown, when you are waiting for dinner to be served. That was Lincoln's method. It has been the method of almost all successful speakers.

4. After you have done a bit of independent thinking, go to the library and do some reading on your topic—if time permits. Tell the librarian your needs. She can render you great assistance.

5. Collect far more material than you intend to use. Imitate Luther Burbank. He often produced a million plant specimens to find one or two superlatively good ones. Assemble a hundred thoughts; discard ninety.

6. The way to develop reserve power is to know far more than you can use, to have a full reservoir of information. In preparing a speech, use the methods Arthur Dunn employed in training his salesmen to sell a breakfast food specialty, the methods that Ida Tarbell employed in preparing her article on the Atlantic cable.

CHAPTER THREE

How Famous Speakers Prepared Their Addresses

I was present once at a luncheon of the New York Rotary Club when the principal speaker was a prominent government official. The high position that he occupied gave him prestige, and we were looking forward with pleasure to hearing him. He had promised to tell us about the activities of his own department; and it was one in which almost every New York business man was interested.

He knew his subject thoroughly, knew far more about it than he could possibly use; but he had not planned his speech. He had not selected his material. He had not arranged it in orderly fashion. Nevertheless, with a courage born of inexperience, he plunged heedlessly, blindly, into his speech. He did not know where he was going, but he was on his way.

His mind was, in short, a mere hodgepodge, and so was the mental feast he served us. He brought on the ice cream first, and then placed the soup before us. Fish and nuts came next. And, on top of that, there was something that seemed to be a mixture of soup and ice cream and good red herring. I have never, anywhere or at any time, seen a speaker more utterly confused.

He had been trying to talk impromptu; but, in desperation now, he drew a bundle of notes out of his pocket, confessing that his secretary had compiled them for him—and no one questioned the veracity of his assertion. The notes themselves evidently had no more order than a flatcar full of scrap iron. He fumbled through them nervously, glancing from one page to another, trying to orient himself, trying to find a way out of the wilderness, and he attempted to talk as he did so. It was impossible. He apologized and, calling for water, took a drink with a trembling hand, uttered a few more scattering sentences, repeated himself, dug into his notes again. . . . Minute by minute he grew more helpless, more lost, more bewildered, more embarrassed. Nervous perspiration stood out on his forehead, and his handkerchief shook as he wiped it away. We in the audience sat watching the fiasco, our sympathies stirred, our feelings harrowed. We suffered positive and vicarious embarrassment. But with more doggedness than discretion, the speaker continued, floundering, studying his notes, apologizing and drinking. Everyone except him felt that the spectacle was rapidly approaching total disaster, and it was a relief to us all when he sat down and ceased his death struggles. It was one of the most uncomfortable audiences I have ever been in; and he was the most ashamed and humiliated speaker I have ever seen. He had made his talk as Rousseau said a love letter should be written: he had begun without knowing what he was going to say, and he had finished without knowing what he had uttered.

The moral of the tale is just this: "When a man's knowledge is not in order," said Herbert Spencer, "the more of it he has, the greater will be his confusion of thought."

No sane man would start to build a house without some sort of plan; but why will he begin to deliver a speech without the vaguest kind of outline or program?

A speech is a voyage with a purpose, and it must be charted. The person who starts nowhere, generally gets there.

I wish that I could paint this saying of Napoleon's in flaming letters of red a foot high over every doorway on the globe where students of public speaking foregather: "The art of war is a science in which nothing succeeds which has not been calculated and thought out."

That is just as true of speaking as of shooting. But do speakers realize it—or, if they do—do they always act on it? They do not. Most emphatically they do not. Many a talk has just a trifle more plan and arrangement than a bowl of fish stew.

What is the best and most effective arrangement for a given set of ideas? No one can say until he has studied them. It is always a new problem, an eternal question that every speaker must ask and answer again and again. No infallible rules can be given; but we can, at any rate, illustrate briefly here, with a concrete case, just what we mean by orderly arrangements.

How a Prize-Winning Speech Was Constructed

Here is a speech that was delivered some years ago before the National Association of Real Estate Boards. It won first prize in competition with twenty-seven other speeches on various cities—and would do so today! This speech is well constructed, full of facts stated clearly, vividly, interestingly. It has spirit. It marches. It will merit reading and study.

Mr. Chairman and Friends:

Back 144 years ago, this great nation, the United States of America, was born in my City of Philadelphia, and so it is quite natural that a city having such an historical record should have that strong American spirit that has not only made it the greatest industrial center in this country, but also one of the largest and most beautiful cities in the whole world.

Philadelphia has a population close to two millions of people, and our city has an area that is equal to the combined size of Milwaukee and Boston, Paris and Berlin, and out of our 130 square miles of territory we have given up nearly 8,000 acres of our best land for beautiful parks, squares and boulevards, so that our people would have the proper places for recreation and pleasure, and the right kind of environment that belongs to every decent American.

Philadelphia, friends, is not only a large, clean and beautiful city, but it is also known everywhere as the great workshop of the world, and the reason it is called the workshop of the world is because we have a vast army of over 400,000 people employed in 9,200 industrial establishments that turn out one hundred thousand dollars' worth of useful commodities every ten minutes of the working day, and according to a well-known statistician, there is no city in this country that equals Philadelphia in the production of woolen goods, leather goods, knit goods, textiles, felt hats, hardware, tools, storage batteries, steel ships and a great many other things. We build a railroad locomotive every two hours day and night, and more than one-half the people in this great country ride in streetcars made in the City of Philadelphia. We manufacture a thousand cigars every minute, and last year, in our 115 hosiery mills, we made two pairs of stockings for every man, woman and child in this country. We make more carpets and rugs than all of Great Britain and Ireland combined, and, in fact, our total commercial and industrial business is so stupendous that our bank clearings last year, amounting to thirty-seven billions of dollars, would have paid for every Liberty Bond in the entire country.

But, friends, while we are very proud of our wonderful industrial progress, and while we are also very proud of being one of the largest medical, art and educational centers in this country, yet, we feel a still greater pride in the fact that we have more individual homes in the City of Philadelphia than there are in any other city in the whole world. In Philadelphia we have 397,000 separate homes, and if these homes were placed on twenty-five-foot lots, side by side, in one single row, that row would reach all the way from Philadelphia clear through to this Convention Hall, at Kansas City, and then on to Denver, a distance of 1,881 miles.

But, what I want to call your special attention to is the significance of the fact that tens of thousands of these homes are owned and occupied by the working people of our city, and when a man owns the ground upon which he stands and the roof over his head, there is no argument ever presented that would infect that man with those imported diseases, known as Socialism and Bolshevism.

Philadelphia is not a fertile soil for European anarchy, because our homes, our educational institutions and our gigantic industry have been produced by that true American spirit that was born in our city, and is a heritage from our forefathers. Philadelphia is the mother city of this great country, and the very fountainhead of American liberty. It is the city where the first American flag was made; it is the city where the first Congress of the United States met; it is the city where the Declaration of Independence was signed; it is the city where that best loved relic in America, the Liberty Bell, has inspired tens of thousands of our men, women and children, so that we believe we have a sacred mission, which is not to worship the golden calf, but to spread the American spirit, and to keep the fires of freedom burning, so that with God's permission, the Government of Washington, Lincoln and Theodore Roosevelt may be an inspiration to all humanity.

Let us analyze that speech. Let us see how it is constructed, how it gets its effects. In the first place, it has a beginning and an ending. That is a rare virtue—more rare than you may be inclined to think. It starts somewhere. It goes there straight as wild geese on the wing. It doesn't dawdle. It loses no time.

It has freshness, individuality. The speaker opens by saying something about his city that the other speakers could not possibly say about theirs: he points out that his city is the birthplace of the entire nation.

He states that it is one of the largest and most beautiful cities in the world. But that claim is general, trite; standing by itself, it would not impress anyone very much. The speaker knew that; so he helped his audience visualize the magnitude of Philadelphia by stating it "has an area equal to the combined size of Milwaukee, Boston, Paris and Berlin." That is definite, concrete. It is interesting. It is surprising. It makes a mark. It drives home the idea better than a whole page of statistics would have done.

Next he declares that Philadelphia is "known everywhere as the great workshop of the world." Sounds exaggerated, doesn't it? Like propaganda. Had he proceeded immediately to the next point no one would have been convinced. But he doesn't. He pauses to enumerate the products in which Philadelphia leads the world: "woolen goods, leather goods, knit goods, textiles, felt hats, hardware, tools, storage batteries, steel ships."

Doesn't sound so much like propaganda now, does it?

Philadelphia "builds a railroad locomotive every two hours day and night, and more than one-half the people in this great country ride in streetcars made in the city of Philadelphia."

"Well, I never knew that," we muse. "Perhaps I rode down town yesterday in one of those streetcars. I'll look to-morrow and see where my town buys its cars."

"A thousand cigars every minute . . . two pairs of stockings for every man, woman and child in this country."

We are still more impressed. . . . "Maybe my favorite cigar is made in Philadelphia . . . and these socks I have on. . . ."

What does the speaker do next? Jump back to the subject of the size of Philadelphia that he covered first and give us some fact that he forgot then? No, not at all. He sticks to a point until he finishes it, has done with it, and need never return to it again. For that we are duly grateful, Mr. Speaker. For what is more confusing and muddling than to have a speaker darting from one thing to another and back again as erratic as a bat in the twilight? Yet many a speaker does just that. Instead of covering his points in order 1, 2, 3, 4, 5, he covers them as a football captain calls out signals—27, 34, 19, 2. No, he is worse than that. He covers them like this—27, 34, 27, 19, 2, 34, 19.

But this speaker, however, steams straight ahead on schedule time, never idling, never turning back, swerving neither to the right nor left, like one of those locomotives he has been talking about.

But, he makes now the weakest point of his entire speech:

Philadelphia, he declares, is "one of the largest medical, art and educational centers in this country." He merely announces that; then speeds on to something else—only twelve words to animate that fact, to make it vivid, to engrave it on the memory. Only twelve words lost, submerged, in a sentence containing a total of sixty-five. It doesn't work. Of course not. The human mind does not operate like a string of steel traps. He devotes so little time to this point, is so general, so vague, seems so unimpressed himself that the effect on the hearer is almost nil. What should be have done? He realized that he could establish this point with the self-same technique that he just employed to establish the fact that Philadelphia is the workshop of the world. He knew that. He also knew that he would have a stop watch held on him during the contest, that he would have five minutes, not a second more; so he had to slur over this point or slight others.

There are "more individual homes in the city of Philadelphia than there are in any other city in the world." How does he make this phase of his topic impressive and convincing? First, he gives the number: 397,000. Second, he visualizes the number: "If these homes were placed on twenty-five-foot lots, side by side, in one single row, that row would reach all the way from Philadelphia clear through this Convention Hall at Kansas City, and then on to Denver, a distance of 1,881 miles."

His audience probably forgot the number he gave before he had finished the sentence. But forget that picture? That would have been well nigh impossible.

So much for cold material facts. But they are not the stuff out of which eloquence is fashioned. This speaker aspired to build up to a climax, to touch the heart, to stir the feelings. So now on the home stretch, he deals with emotional material. He tells what the ownership of those homes means to the spirit of the city. He denounces "those imported diseases, known as Socialism and Bolshevism." He eulogizes Philadelphia as "the very fountainhead of American liberty." Liberty! A magic word, a word full of feeling, a sentiment for which millions have laid down their lives. That phrase in itself is good, but it is a thousand times better when he backs it up with concrete references to historic events and documents, dear, sacred, to the hearts of his hearers. . . . "It is the city where the first American Flag was made; it is the city where the first Congress of the United States met; it is the city where the Declaration of Independence was signed . . . Liberty Bell . . . a sacred mission . . . , to spread the American spirit . . . to keep the fires of freedom burning, so that with God's permission, the Government of Washington, Lincoln and Theodore Roosevelt may be an inspiration to all humanity." That is a real climax!

So much for the composition of this talk. But admirable as it is from the standpoint of construction, this speech could come to grief, could easily have been brought to naught, had it been expressed in a calm manner devoid of all spirit and vitality. But the speaker delivered it as he composed it, with a feeling and enthusiasm born of the deepest sincerity. Small wonder that it won first prize, that it was awarded the Chicago cup.

The Way Doctor Conwell Planned His Speeches

There are not, as I have already said, any infallible rules that will solve the question of the best arrangement. There are no designs or schemes or charts that will fit all or even a majority of speeches; yet here are a few speech plans that will prove usable in some instances. The late Dr. Russell H. Conwell, the author of the famous "Acres of Diamonds," once informed me that he had built many of his innumerable speeches on this outline:

1. State your facts.
2. Argue from them.
3. Appeal for action.

Many people have found this plan very helpful and stimulating:

1. Show something that is wrong.
2. Show how to remedy it.
3. Ask for coöperation.

Or, to put it in another way:

1. Here is a situation that ought to be remedied.
2. We ought to do so and so about the matter.
3. You ought to help for these reasons.

This outline is briefly still another speech plan:

1. Secure interested attention.
2. Win confidence.
3. State your facts; educate people regarding the merits of your proposition.
4. Appeal to the motives that make men act.

How Famous Men Have Built a Talk

Former Senator Albert J. Beveridge wrote a very short and very practical book entitled *The Art of Public Speaking.* "The speaker must be master of his subject," said this noted political campaigner. "That means that all the facts must be collected, arranged, studied, digested—not only data on one side, but material on the other side and on every side—all of it. And be sure that they are facts, not mere assumptions or unproved assertions. Take nothing for granted.

"Therefore check up and verify every item. This means painstaking research, to be sure, but what of it?—are you not proposing to inform, instruct, and advise your fellow citizens? Are you not setting yourself up as an authority?

"Having assembled and marshalled the facts of any problem, *think out for yourself the solution those facts compel.* Thus your speech will have originality and personal force—it will be vital and compelling. There will be *you* in it. Then write out your ideas as clearly and logically as you can."

In other words, present the facts on both sides, and then present the conclusion that those facts make clear and definite.

"I begin," said Woodrow Wilson when asked to explain his methods, "with a list of the topics I want to cover, *arranging them in my mind in their natural relations*—that is, I fit the bones of the thing together; then I write it out in shorthand. I have always been accustomed to writing in shorthand, finding it a great saver of time. This done, I copy it on my own typewriter, changing phrases, correcting sentences, and adding material as I go along."

Theodore Roosevelt prepared his talks in the characteristic Rooseveltian manner: he dug up all the facts, reviewed them, appraised them, determined their findings, arrived at his conclusions, arrived with a feeling of certainty that was unshakable.

Then, with a pad of notes before him, he started dictating and he dictated his speech very rapidly so that it would have rush and spontaneity and the spirit of life. Then he went over this typewritten copy, revised it, inserted, deleted, filled it with pencil marks, and then dictated it all over again. "I never won anything," said he, "without hard labor and the exercise of my best judgment and careful planning and working long in advance."

Often he called in critics to listen to him as he dictated or read his speech to them. He refused to debate with them the wisdom of what he had said. His mind was already made up on that point, and made up irrevocably. He wanted to be told, not what to say, but how to say it. Again and again he went over his typewritten copies, cutting, correcting, improving. That was the speech that the newspapers printed. Of course, he did not memorize it. He spoke extemporaneously. So the talk actually delivered often differed somewhat from the published and polished one. But the task of dictating and revising was excellent preparation. It made him familiar with his material, with the order of his points. It gave him a smoothness and sureness and polish that he could hardly have obtained in any other fashion.

Sir Oliver Lodge told me that dictating his talks—dictating them rapidly and with substance, dictating them just as if he were actually talking to an audience—he had discovered to be an excellent means of preparation and practice.

Many students of speech have found it illuminating to

dictate their talks to the dictaphone, and then to listen to themselves. Illuminating? Yes, and sometimes disillusioning and chastening also, I fear. It is a most wholesome exercise. I recommend it.

This practice of actually writing out what you are going to say, will force you to think. It will clarify your ideas. It will hook them in your memory. It will reduce your mental wandering to a minimum. It will improve your diction.

Benjamin Franklin tells in his *Autobiography* how he improved his diction, how he developed readiness in using words, and how he taught himself method in arranging his thoughts. This story of his life is a literary classic, and, unlike most classics, it is easy to read and thoroughly enjoyable. It is almost a model of plain, straightforward English. Every would-be speaker and writer can peruse it with pleasure and profit. I think you will like the selection I refer to; here it is:

> About this time I met with an odd volume of the Spectator. It was the third. I had never before seen any of them. I bought it, read it over and over and was much delighted with it. I thought the writing excellent, and wished, if possible, to imitate it. With this view I took some of the papers, and, making short hints of the sentiment in each sentence laid them by a few days, and then, without looking at the book, try'd to compleat the papers again, by expressing each hinted sentiment at length, and as fully as it had been expressed before, in any suitable words that should come to hand. Then I compared my Spectator with the original, discovered some of my faults and corrected them. But I found a stock of words, and a readiness in recollecting and using them, which I thought I should have acquired before that time if I had gone on making verses; since the continual occasion for words of the same import, but of different length, to suit the measure, or of different sounds for the rhyme, would have laid me under a constant necessity of searching for variety, and also have tended to fix that variety in my mind, and make me master of it. Therefore I took some of the tales and turned them back again. I also sometimes jumbled my

collections of hints into confusion, and after some weeks endeavored to reduce them into the best order, before I began to form the full sentences and compleat the paper. *This was to teach me method in the arrangement of thoughts.* By comparing my work afterwards with the original, I discovered many faults and amended them; but I sometimes had the pleasure of fancying that, in certain particulars of small import, I had been lucky enough to improve the method of the language, and this encouraged me to think I might possibly in time come to be a tolerable English writer, of which I was extremely ambitious.

Play Solitaire with Your Notes

You were advised in the last chapter to make notes. Having gotten your various ideas and illustrations down on scraps of paper, play solitaire with them—toss them into series of related piles. These main piles ought to represent, approximately, the main points of your talk. Subdivide them into smaller lots. Throw out the chaff until there is nothing but number one wheat left—and even some of the wheat will probably have to be put aside and not used. No one, if he works right, is ever able to use but a percentage of the material he gathers.

One ought never to cease this process of revision until the speech has been made—even then he is very likely to think of points and improvements and refinements that ought to have been made.

A good speaker usually finds when he finishes that there have been four versions of his speech: the one that he prepared, the one that he delivered, the one that the newspapers said that he delivered, and the one that he wishes, on his way home, that he had delivered.

"Shall I Use Notes While Speaking?"

Although he was an excellent impromptu speaker, Lincoln, after he reached the White House, never made any address, not even an informal talk to his cabinet, until he had carefully put it all down in writing beforehand. Of course, he was obliged to read his inaugural addresses. The exact phraseology of historical state papers of that character is too important to be left to extemporizing. But, back in Illinois, Lincoln never used even notes in his speaking. "They always tend to tire and confuse the listener," he said.

And who of us, pray, would contradict him? Don't notes destroy about fifty per cent of your interest in a talk? Don't they prevent, or at least render difficult, a very precious contact and intimacy that ought to exist between the speaker and the audience? Don't they create an air of artificiality? Don't they restrain an audience from feeling that the speaker has the confidence and reserve power that he or she ought to have?

Make notes, I repeat, during the preparation—elaborate ones, profuse ones. You may wish to refer to them when you are practicing your talk alone. You may possibly feel more comfortable if you have them stored away in your pocket when you are facing an audience; but, like the hammer and saw and axe in a Pullman coach, they should be emergency tools, only for use in the case of a smash-up, a total wreck, and threatening death and disaster.

If you must use notes, make them extremely brief and write them in large letters on an ample sheet of paper. Then arrive early at the place where you are to speak and hide your notes behind some books on a table. Glance at them when you must, but endeavor to screen your weakness from the audience.

However, in spite of all that has been said there may be times when it is the part of wisdom to use notes. For example, some people during their first few talks, are so nervous and self-conscious that they are utterly unable to remember their prepared speeches. The result? They shoot off at a tangent; they forget the material they had so carefully rehearsed; they drift off the high road and flounder about in a morass. Why should not such persons hold a few very condensed notes in their hands during their maiden efforts? A child clutches the furniture when it is first attempting to walk; but it does not continue it very long.

Do Not Memorize Verbatim

Don't read, and don't attempt to memorize your talk word for word. That consumes time, and courts disaster. Yet, in spite of this warning, some people reading these lines will try it; if they do, when they stand up to speak they will be thinking of what? Of their messages? No, they will be attempting to recall their exact phraseology. They will be thinking backward, not forward, reversing the usual processes of the human mind. The whole exhibition will be stiff and cold and colorless and inhuman. Do not, I beg of you, waste hours and energy in such futility.

When you have an important business interview, do you sit down and memorize, verbatim, what you are going to say? Do you? Of course not. You reflect until you get your main ideas clearly in mind. You may make a few notes and consult some records. You say to yourself: "I shall bring out this point and that. I am going to say that a certain thing ought to be done for these reasons. . . ." Then you enumerate the reasons to yourself and illustrate them with concrete cases. Isn't that the way you prepare for a business interview? Why not use the same common sense method in preparing a talk?

Grant at Appomattox

When Lee asked Grant to write down the terms of surrender, the leader of the Union forces turned to General Parker, asking for writing material. "When I put my pen to paper," Grant records in his *Memoirs,* "I did not know the first word I should make use of in writing the terms. I only knew what was in my mind, and I wished to express it clearly, so there could be no mistaking it."

General Grant, you did not need to know the first word. You had ideas. You had convictions. You had something that you very much wanted to say and to say clearly. The result was that your habitual phraseology came tumbling out without conscious effort. The same holds good for any man. If you doubt it, knock a man down; when he gets up, he will discover that he is hardly at a loss to find words to express himself.

Two thousand years ago, Horace wrote:

> Seek not for words, seek only fact and thought,
> And crowding in will come the words unsought.

After you have your ideas firmly in mind, then rehearse your talk from beginning to end. Do it silently, mentally, as you watch for the teakettle to boil, as you walk the street, as you wait for the elevator. Get off in a room by yourself and go over it aloud, gesturing, saying it with life and energy. Canon Knox Little, of Canterbury, used to say a preacher never got the real message out of a sermon until he had preached it half a dozen times. Can you hope, then, to get the real message out of your talk unless you have at least rehearsed it that many times? As you practice, imagine there is a real audience before you. Imagine it so strongly that when there is one, it will seem like an old experience.

Why the Farmers Thought Lincoln "Awfully Lazy"

If you practice your talks in this fashion, you will be faithfully following the examples of many famous speakers. Lloyd George, when he was a member of a debating society in his home town in Wales, often strolled along the country lanes, talking and gesturing to the trees and fence posts.

Lincoln, in his younger days, often walked a round trip of thirty or forty miles to hear a famous speaker like Breckenridge. He came home from these scenes so stirred, so determined to be a speaker that he gathered the other hired workers about him in the fields and, mounting a stump, he made speeches and told them stories. His employers grew angry, declaring that this country Cicero was "awfully lazy," that his jokes and his oratory were ruining the rest of the workers.

Asquith gained his first facility by becoming an active worker in the Union Debating Society in Oxford. Later he organized one of his own. Woodrow Wilson learned to speak in a debating society. So did Henry Ward Beecher. So did the mighty Burke. So did Antoinette Blackwell and Lucy Stone. Elihu Root practiced before a literary society in the Twenty-Third Street YMCA in New York.

Study the careers of famous speakers and you will find one fact that is true of them all: *they practiced.* THEY PRACTICED. And the men who make the most rapid progress in this course are those who practice most.

No time for all this? Then do what Joseph Choate used to do. He bought a newspaper of a morning and buried his head in it as he rode to work so no one would bother him. Then, instead of reading the ephemeral scandals and gossip of the day, he thought out and planned his talks.

Chauncey M. Depew led a fairly active life as a railroad president and a United States Senator. Yet, during it all, he made speeches almost every night. "I did not let them interfere with my business," he says. "They were all prepared after I had arrived home from my office late in the afternoon."

We all have several hours a day that we can do with as we please. That was all Darwin had to work with, as he had poor health. Three hours out of twenty-four, wisely used, made him famous.

Theodore Roosevelt, when he was in the White House, often had an entire forenoon given over to a series of five-minute interviews. Yet he kept a book by his side to utilize even the few spare seconds that came between his engagements.

If you are very busy and pushed for time, read Arnold Bennett's *How to Live on Twenty-four Hours a Day.* Rip out a hundred pages, put them in your hip pocket, read them during your spare seconds. I got through the book in two days in that fashion. It will show you how to save time, how to get more out of the day.

You must have relaxation and a change from your regular

work. That is what the practicing of your talks ought to be. Play the game of extemporaneous speaking in your own home with your own family.

Summary

1. "The art of war," said Napoleon, "is a science in which nothing succeeds which has not been calculated and thought out." That is as true of speaking as of shooting. A talk is a voyage. It must be charted. The speaker who starts nowhere, usually gets there.

2. No infallible, ironclad rules can be given for the arrangement of ideas and the construction of all talks. Each address presents it own particular problems.

3. The speaker should cover a point thoroughly while he is on it, and then not refer to it again. As an illustration, see the prize-winning address on Philadelphia. There should be no darting from one thing to another and then back again as aimlessly as a bat in the twilight.

4. The late Dr. Conwell built many of his talks on this plan:

   a. State your facts.
   b. Argue from them.
   c. Appeal for action.

5. You will probably find this plan very helpful:

   a. Show something that is wrong.
   b. Show how to remedy it.
   c. Appeal for action.

6. Here is an excellent speech plan:

   a. Secure interested attention.
   b. Win confidence.
   c. State your facts.
   d. Appeal to the motives that make men act.

7. "All the facts on both sides of your subject," advised former Senator Albert J. Beveridge, "must be collected, arranged, studied, digested. Prove them; be sure they are

facts; then think out for yourself the solution those facts compel."

8. Before speaking, Lincoln thought out his conclusions with mathematical exactness. When he was forty years of age, and after he had been a member of Congress, he studied Euclid so that he could detect sophistry and demonstrate his conclusions.

9. When Theodore Roosevelt was preparing a speech, he dug up all the facts, appraised them, then dictated his speech very rapidly, corrected the typewritten copy, and finally dictated it all over again.

10. If possible, dictate your talk to a dictaphone and listen to it.

11. Notes destroy about fifty per cent of the interest in your talk. Avoid them. Above all, do not read your talk. An audience can hardly be brought to endure listening to a read speech.

12. After you have thought out and arranged your talk, then practice it silently as you walk along the street. Also get off somewhere by yourself and go over it from beginning to end, using gestures, letting yourself go. Imagine that you are addressing a real audience. The more of this you do, the more comfortable you will feel when the time comes for you to make your talk.

CHAPTER FOUR

The Improvement of Memory

"The average man," said the noted psychologist, Professor Carl Seashore, "does not use above ten per cent of his actual inherited capacity for memory. He wastes the ninety per cent by violating the natural laws of remembering."

Are you one of these average persons? If so, you are struggling under a handicap both socially and commercially; consequently, you will be interested in, and profit by, reading and rereading this chapter. It describes and explains these natural laws of remembering and shows how to use them in business and social conversation as well as in public speaking.

These "natural laws of remembering" are very simple. There are only three. Every so-called "memory system" has been founded upon them. Briefly, they are *impression, repetition,* and *association.*

The first mandate of memory is this: get a deep, vivid and lasting *impression* of the thing you wish to retain. And to do that, you must concentrate. Theodore Roosevelt's remarkable memory impressed everyone he met. And no little amount of his extraordinary facility was due to this: his impressions were scratched on steel, not written in water. He had, by persistence and practice, trained himself to concentrate under the most adverse conditions. In 1912, during the Bull Moose Convention in Chicago, his headquarters were in the Congress Hotel. Crowds surged through the street below, crying, waving banners, shouting "We want Teddy! We want Teddy!" The roar of the throng, the music of bands, the coming and going of politicians, the hurried conferences, the consultations—would have driven the ordinary individual to distraction; but Roosevelt sat in a rocking chair in his room, oblivious to it all, reading Herodotus, the Greek historian. On his trip through the Brazilian wilderness, as soon as he reached the camping ground in the evening, he found a dry spot under some huge tree, got out a camp stool and his copy of Gibbon's "Decline and Fall of the Roman Empire," and, at once, he was so immersed in the book that he was oblivious to the rain, to the noise and activity of the camp, to the sounds of the tropical forest. Small wonder that the man remembered what he read.

Five minutes of vivid, energetic concentration will produce greater results than days of mooning about in a mental haze. "One intense hour," wrote Henry Ward Beecher, "will do more than dreamy years." "If there is any one thing that I have learned which is more important than anything else," said Eugene Grace, who made over a million a year as president of Bethlehem Steel Company, "and which I practice every day under any and all circumstances, it is *concentration in the particular job I have in hand.*"

This is one of the secrets of power, especially memory power.

They Coudn't See a Cherry Tree

Thomas Edison found that twenty-seven of his assistants had used, every day for six months, a certain path which led from his lamp factory to the main works at Menlo Park, New Jersey. A cherry tree grew along that path, and yet not one of these twenty-seven men had, when questioned, ever been conscious of that tree's existence.

"The average person's brain," declared Mr. Edison with heat and energy, "does not observe a thousandth part of what the eye observes. It is almost incredible how poor our powers of observation—genuine observation—are."

Introduce the average person to two or three of your friends and, the chances are that two minutes afterward he cannot recall the name of a single one of them. And why? Because he never paid sufficient attention to them in the first place, he never accurately observed them. He will likely tell you he has a poor memory. No, he has a poor observation. He would not condemn a camera because it failed to take pictures in a fog, but he expects his mind to retain impressions that are hazy and foggy to a degree. Of course, it can't be done.

Joseph Pulitzer, who made the *New York World,* had three words placed over the desk of every man in his editorial offices:

Accuracy
ACCURACY
ACCURACY

That is what we want. Hear the man's name precisely. Insist on it. Ask him to repeat it. Inquire how it is spelled. He will be flattered by your interest and you will be able to remember his name because you have concentrated on it. You have got a clear, accurate impression.

Why Lincoln Read Aloud

Lincoln, in his youth, attended a country school where the floor was made out of split logs: greased pages, torn from the copybooks and pasted over the windows, served instead of glass to let in the light. Only one copy of the textbook existed, and the teacher read from it aloud. The pupils repeated the lesson after him, all of them talking at once. It made a constant uproar, and the neighbors called it the "blab school."

At the "blab school," Lincoln formed a habit that clung to him all his life: he forever read aloud everything he wished to remember. Each morning, as soon as he reached his law office in Springfield, he spread himself out on the couch, hooked one long, ungainly leg over a neighboring chair, and read the newspaper audibly. "He annoyed me," said his partner, "almost beyond endurance. I once asked him why he read in this fashion. This was his explanation: 'When I read aloud, two senses catch the idea: first, I see what I read; second, I hear it, and therefore I can remember it better.' "

His memory was extraordinarily retentive. "My mind," he said, "is like a piece of steel—very hard to scratch anything on it, but almost impossible, after you get it there, to rub it out."

Appealing to two of the senses was the method he used to do the scratching. Go thou, and do likewise. . . .

The ideal thing would be not only to see and hear the thing to be remembered, but to touch it, and smell it, and taste it.

But, above all else, see it. We are visual minded. Eye impressions stick. We can often remember a man's face, even though we cannot recall his name. The nerves that lead from the eye to the brain are twenty-five times as large as those leading from the ear to the brain. The Chinese have a proverb that says "one time seeing is worth a thousand times hearing."

Write down the name, the telephone number, the speech outline you want to remember. Look at it. Close your eyes. Visualize it in flaming letters of fire.

How Mark Twain Learned to Speak Without Notes

The discovery of how to use his visual memory enabled Mark Twain to discard the notes that had hampered his speeches for years. Here is his story as he told it in *Harper's Magazine:*

> Dates are hard to remember because they consist of figures: figures are monotonously unstriking in appearance, and they don't take hold; they form no pictures, and so they give the eye no chance to take hold. Pictures can make dates stick. They can make nearly anything stick—particularly if you make the picture yourself. Indeed, that is the great point—make the picture yourself. I know about this from experience. Thirty years ago I was delivering a memorized lecture every night, and every night I had to help myself with a page of notes to keep from getting myself mixed. The notes consisted of beginnings of sentences, and were eleven in number, and they ran something like this:
>
> In that region the weather—
>
> At that time it was a custom—
>
> But in California one never heard—
>
> Eleven of them. They initialed the brief of the lecture and protected me against skipping. But they all looked about alike on the page; they formed no picture; I had them by heart, but I could never with certainty remember the order of their succession; therefore, I always had to keep those notes by me and look at them every little while. Once I mislaid them; you will not be able to imagine the terrors of that evening. I now saw that I must invent some other protection. So I got ten of the initial letters by heart in their proper order—I, A, B, and so on—and I went on the platform the next night with these marked in ink on my ten finger nails. But it didn't answer. I kept track of the fingers for awhile; then I lost it, and after that I was never quite sure which finger I had used last. I couldn't lick off a letter after using it, for while that would have made success certain, it would also have provoked too much curiosity. There was curiosity enough without that. To the audience I seemed more interested in my finger nails than I was in my subject; one or two persons asked afterward what was the matter with my hands.
>
> It was then that the idea of pictures occurred to me!

Then my troubles passed away. In two minutes I made six pictures with my pen, and they did the work of the eleven catch-sentences and did it perfectly. I threw the pictures away as soon as they were made, for I was sure I could shut my eyes and see them any time. That was a quarter of a century ago; the lecture vanished out of my head more than twenty years ago, but I could rewrite it from the pictures—for they remain.

I had occasion to deliver a talk on memory. I wanted to use, very largely, the material in this chapter. I memorized the points by pictures. I visualized Roosevelt reading history while the crowds were yelling and bands playing outside his window. I saw Thomas Edison looking at a cherry tree. I pictured Lincoln reading a newspaper aloud. I imagined Mark Twain licking ink off his fingernails as he faced an audience.

How did I remember the order of the pictures? By one, two, three, and four? No, that would have been too difficult. I turned these numbers into pictures, and combined the pictures of the numbers with the pictures of the points. To illustrate. Number *one* sounds like *run,* so I made a race horse stand for *one.* I pictured Roosevelt in his room, reading astride a race horse. For *two,* I chose a word that sounds like two—*zoo.* I had the cherry tree that Thomas Edison was looking at standing in the bear cage at the zoo. For *three,* I pictured an object that sounds like three—*tree.* I had Lincoln sprawled out in the top of a tree, reading aloud to his partner. For *four* I imagined a picture that sounds like four—*door.* Mark Twain stood in an open door, leaning against the jamb, licking the ink off his fingers as he talked to the audience.

I realize full well that many men who read this will think that such a method verges on the ridiculous. It does. That is one reason why it works. It is comparatively easy to remember the bizarre and ridiculous. Had I tried to remember the order of my points by numbers only, I might easily have forgotten; but by the system I have just described, it was almost impossible to forget. When I wished to recall my third point, I had but to ask myself what was in the top of the tree. Instantly I saw Lincoln.

I have, very largely for my own convenience, turned the numbers from one to twenty into pictures, choosing pictures that sound like the numbers. I have set them down here. If you will spend half an hour memorizing these picture-numerals you will then be able, after having a list of twenty objects called to you but once, to repeat them in their exact order and to skip about at random announcing which object was called to you eighth, which fourteenth, which third, and so on.

Here are the picture numbers. Try the test. You will find it decidedly amusing.

1. Run—visualize a race horse.

2. Zoo—see the bear cage in the zoo.

3. Tree—picture the third object called to you as lying in the top of a tree.

4. Door—or wild boar. Take any object or animal that sounds like four.

5. Bee hive.

6. Sick—see a Red Cross nurse.

7. Heaven—a street paved with gold, and angels playing on harps.

8. Gate.

9. Wine—the bottle has fallen over on the table, and the wine is streaming out and pouring down something below. Put action into the pictures. It helps to make them stick.

10. Den of wild animals in a rocky cave in the deep woods.

11. A football eleven, rushing madly across the field. I picture them carrying aloft the object that I wish to recall as number eleven.

12. Shelve—see some one shoving something back on a shelf.

13. Hurting—see the blood spurting out of a wound and reddening the thirteenth object.

14. Courting—a couple are sitting on something and making love.

15. Lifting—a strong man, a regular John L. Sullivan, is lifting something high above his head.

16. Licking—a fist fight.

17. Leavening—a housewife is kneading dough, and into the dough she kneads the seventeenth object.

18. Waiting—a woman is standing at a forked path in the deep woods waiting for some one.

19. Pining—a woman is weeping. See her tears falling on the nineteenth thing you wish to recall.

20. Horn of Plenty—a goat's horn overflowing with flowers and fruit and corn.

If you wish to try the test, spend a few minutes memorizing these picture-numbers. If you prefer, make pictures of your own. For ten, think of *wren* or fountain *pen* or *hen* or *sen-sen*—anything that sounds like ten. Suppose that the tenth object recalled to you a windmill. See the hen sitting on the windmill, or see it pumping ink to fill the fountain pen. Then, when you are asked what was the tenth object called, do not think of ten at all; but merely ask yourself where was the hen sitting. You may not think it will work, but try it. You can soon astound people with what they will consider to be an extraordinary capacity for remembering. You will find it entertaining if nothing else.

Memorizing a Book as Long as the New Testament

One of the largest universities in the world is the Al-Azhar at Cairo. It is a Mohammedan institution with twenty-one thousand students. The entrance examination requires every applicant to repeat the Koran from memory. The Koran is about as long as the New Testament, and three days are required to recite it!

The Chinese students, or "study boys" as they are called, have to memorize some of the religious and classical books of China.

How are these Arab and Chinese students able to perform these apparently prodigious feats of memory?

By *repetition,* the second "natural law of remembering."

You can memorize an almost endless amount of material if you will repeat it often enough. Go over the knowledge you want to remember. Use it. Apply it. Employ the new word in your conversation. Call the stranger by his name if you want to remember it. Talk over in conversation the points you want to make in your public address. The knowledge that is used tends to stick.

The Kind of Repetition That Counts

But the mere blind, mechanical going over a thing by rote is not enough. Intelligent repetition, repetition done in accordance with certain well-established traits of the mind—that is what we must have. For example, Professor Ebbinghaus gave his students a long list of nonsense syllables to memorize, such as "deyux," "qoli," and so on. He found that these students memorized as many of these syllables by thirty-eight repetitions, distributed over a period of three days, as they did by sixty-eight repetitions done at a single sitting. . . . Other psychological tests have repeatedly shown similar results.

That is a very significant discovery about the working of our memories. It means that we know now that the man who sits down and repeats a thing over and over until he finally fastens it in his memory, is using twice as much time and energy as is necessary to achieve the same results when the repeating process is done at judicious intervals.

This peculiarity of the mind—if we can call it such—can be explained by two factors:

First, during the intervals between repetitions, our subconscious minds are busy making the associations more secure. As Professor James sagely remarks: "We learn to swim during the winter and to skate during the summer."

Second, the mind, coming to the task at intervals, is not fatigued by the strain of an unbroken application. Sir Richard Burton, the translator of the "Arabian Nights," spoke twenty-seven languages like a native: yet he confessed that he never studied or practiced any language for more than fifteen minutes at a time, "for, after that, the brain lost its freshness."

Surely, now, in the face of these facts, no man who prides himself on his common sense will delay the preparation of a talk until the night before it is to be given. If he does, his memory will, of necessity, be working at only one-half its possible efficiency.

Here is a very helpful discovery about the way in which we forget. Psychological experiments have repeatedly shown that of the new material we have learned, we forget more during the first eight hours than during the next thirty days. An amazing ratio! So, immediately before you go into a business conference or a PTA meeting or a club group, immediately before you make a speech, look over your data, think over your facts, refresh your memory.

Lincoln knew the value of such a practice, and employed it. The scholarly Edward Everett preceded him on the program of speech making at Gettysburg. When he saw that Everett was approaching the close of his long, formal oration, Lincoln "grew visibly nervous, as he always did when another man was speaking and he was to follow." Hastily adjusting his spectacles, he took his manuscript from his pocket and read it silently to himself to refresh his memory.

Professor William James Explains the Secret of a Good Memory

So much for the first two laws of remembering. The third one, *association,* however, is the indispensable element in recalling. In fact, it is the explanation of memory itself. "Our mind is," as Professor James sagely observed, "essentially an associating machine. . . . Suppose I am silent for a moment, and then say in commanding accents: 'Remember! Recollect!' Does your faculty of memory obey the order, and reproduce any definite image from your past? Certainly not. It stands staring into vacancy, and asking, 'What kind of thing do you wish me to remember?' It needs, in short, a cue. But, if I say, remember the date of your birth, or remember what you had for breakfast, or remember the succession of notes in the musical scale; then your faculty of memory immediately produces the required result: the *cue* determines its vast set of potentialities toward a particular point. And if you now look to see how this happens, you immediately perceive that the *cue* is something contiguously associated with the thing recalled. The words, 'date of my birth,' have an ingrained association with a particular number, month, and year; the words, 'breakfast this morning,' cut off all other lines of recall except those which lead to coffee and bacon and eggs; the words, 'musical scale,' are inveterate mental neighbors of do, re, mi, fa, sol, la, si, do. The laws of association govern, in fact, all the trains of our thinking which are not interrupted by sensations breaking on us from without. Whatever appears in the mind must be *introduced;* and, when introduced, it is as the associate of something already there. This is as true of what you are recollecting as it is of everything else you think of . . . . An educated memory depends upon an organized system of associations; and its goodness depends on two of their peculiarities: first, on the persistency of the associations; and, second, on their number. . . . The 'secret of a good memory' is thus the secret of forming diverse and multiple associations with every fact we care to retain. But this forming of associations with a fact—what is it but thinking about the fact as much as possible? Briefly, then, of two men with the same outward experiences, *the one who thinks over his experiences most,* and weaves them into the most systematic relations with each other, will be the one with the best memory."

How to Link Your Facts Together

Very good, but how are we to set about weaving our facts into systematic relations with each other? The answer is this: by finding their meaning, by thinking them over. For example, if you will ask and answer these questions about any new fact, that process will help to weave it into a systematic relation with other facts:

a. Why is this so?

b. How is this so?

c. When is it so?

d. Where is it so?

e. Who said it is so?

If it is a stranger's name, for example, and it is a common one, we can perhaps tie it to some friend who bears the same name. On the other hand, if it is unusual, we can take occasion to say so. This often leads the stranger to talk about his name. For example: while writing this chapter, I was introduced to a Mrs. Soter. I requested her to spell the name and remarked upon its unusualness. "Yes," she replied, "it is very uncommon. It is a Greek word meaning 'the Saviour'." Then she told me about her husband's people who had come from Athens and of the high positions they had held in the government there. I have found it quite easy to get people to talk about their names, and it always helps me to remember them.

Observe the stranger's looks sharply. Note the color of his eyes and his hair, and look closely at his features. Note how he is dressed. Listen to his manner of talking. Get a clear, keen, vivid impression of his looks and personality, and associate these with his name. The next time these sharp impressions return to your mind, they will help bring the name with them.

Haven't you had the experience, when meeting a man for the second or third time, of discovering that although you could remember his business or profession, you could not recall his name? The reason is this: a man's business is something definite and concrete. It has a meaning. It will adhere like a court plaster while his meaningless name will roll away like hail falling on a steep roof. Consequently, to make sure of your ability to recall a man's name, fashion a phrase about it that will tie it up to his business. There can be no doubt whatever about the efficacy of this method. For example, twenty men, strangers to one another, recently met in the Penn Athletic Club of Philadelphia. Each man was asked to rise, announce his name and business. A phrase was then manufactured to connect the two; and, within a few minutes, each person present could repeat the name of every other individual in the room. Many meetings later, neither the names nor businesses were forgotten, for they were linked together. They adhered.

Here are the first few names, in alphabetical order, from that group; and here are the crude phrases that were used to tie the names to the businesses:

Mr. G. P. Albrecht (Sand business)—"Sand makes all bright."

Mr. G. W. Bayless (Asphalt)—"Use asphalt and pay less."

Mr. H. M. Biddle (Woolen cloth)—"Mr. Biddle piddles about the wool business."

Mr. Gideon Boericke (Mining)—"Boericke bores quickly for mines."

Mr. Thomas Devery (Printing)—"Every man needs Devery's printing."

Mr. O. W. Doolittle (Automobiles)—"Do little and you won't succeed in selling cars."

Mr. Thomas Fischer (Coal)—"He fishes for coal orders."

Mr. Frank H. Goldey (Lumber)—"There is gold in the lumber business."

Mr. J. H. Hancock (Saturday Evening Post)—"Sign your John Hancock to a subscription blank for the *Saturday Evening Post.*"

How to Remember Dates

Dates can best be retained by connecting them with important dates already firmly established in the mind. Isn't it far more difficult, for example, for an American to remember that the Suez Canal was opened in 1869 than to remember that the first ship passed through it four years after the close of the Civil War? If an American tried to remember that the first settlement in Australia was made in 1788, the date is likely to drop out of his mind like a loose bolt out of a car; it is far more likely to stick if he thinks of it in connection with July 4, 1776, and remembers that it occurred twelve years after the Declaration of Independence. That is like screwing a nut on the loose bolt. It holds.

It is well to bear this principle in mind when you are selecting a telephone number. For example, the writer's phone number, during the war, was 1776. No one had difficulty in remembering it. If you can secure from the phone company some such number as 1492, 1861, 1865, 1914, 1918, your friends will not have to consult the directory. They might forget that your phone number was 1492, if you gave them the information in a colorless fashion; but would it slip their minds if you said, "You can easily remember my phone number: 1492, the year Columbus discovered America"?

The Australians, New Zealanders, and Canadians who are reading these lines would, of course, substitute for 1776, 1861, 1865 significant dates in their own history.

What is the best way to memorize the following dates?

a. 1564—Birth of Shakespeare.

b. 1607—The first English settlement in America was made in Jamestown.

c. 1819—The birth of Queen Victoria.

d. 1807—The birth of Robert E. Lee.

e. 1789—The Bastille was destroyed.

You would doubtless find it tiresome to memorize, by sheer mechanical repetition, the names of the thirteen original states in the order in which they entered the Union. But tie them together with a story and the memorizing can be done with a fraction of the time and trying. Read the following paragraph just once. Concentrate. When you have finished, see if you cannot name the thirteen states in their correct order:

> One Saturday afternoon a young lady from Delaware bought a ticket over the Pennsylvania railroad for a little outing. She packed a New Jersey sweater in her suitcase, and visited a friend, Georgia, in Connecticut. The next morning the hostess and her visitor attended Mass in a church on Mary's land. Then they took the South car line home, and dined on a new ham, which had been roasted by Virginia, the colored cook, from New York. After dinner they took the North car line and rode to the island.

How to Remember the Points of Your Talk

There are only two ways by which we can possibly think of a thing: first, by means of an *outside stimulus;* second, by *association* with something already in the mind. Applied to speeches, that means just this: first, you can recall your points by the aid of some outside stimulus such as notes—but who likes to see a speaker use notes? Second, you can remember your points by associating them with something already in the mind. They should be arranged in such a logical order that the first one leads inevitably to the second, and the second to the third as naturally as the door of one room leads into another.

That sounds simple, but it may not prove so for the beginner whose thinking powers are rendered *hors de combat* with fear. There is, however, a method of tying your points together that is easy, rapid, and all but foolproof. I refer to the use of a nonsense sentence. To illustrate: suppose you wish to discuss a veritable jumble of ideas, unassociated and hence hard to remember, such as, for example, *cow, cigar, Napoleon, house, religion.* Let us see if we cannot weld those ideas like the links of a chain by means of this absurd sentence: "The cow smoked a cigar and hooked Napoleon, and the house burned down with religion."

Now, will you please cover the sentence above with your hand while you answer these questions? What is the third point in that talk; the fifth; fourth; second; first?

Does the method work? It does! And you who are trying to improve your memory are urged to use it.

Any group of ideas can be linked together in some such fashion, and the more ridiculous the sentence used for the linking, the easier it will be to recall.

What to Do in Case of a Complete Breakdown

Let us suppose that, in spite of all her preparation and precaution, a speaker, in the middle of her talk before a church group, suddenly finds her mind a blank—suddenly finds herself staring at her hearers completely balked, unable to go on—a terrifying situation. Her pride rebels at sitting down in confusion and defeat. She feels that she might be able to think of her next point, of some point, if she had only ten, fifteen seconds of grace; but even fifteen seconds of frantic silence before an audience would be little less than disastrous. What is to be done? When a certain well-known U. S. Senator recently found himself in this situation he asked his audience if he were speaking loudly enough, if he could be heard distinctly in the back of the room. He knew that he was. He was not seeking information. He was seeking time. And in that momentary pause, he grasped his thought and proceeded.

But perhaps the best lifesaver in such a mental hurricane is this: use the last word, or phrase, or idea in your last sentence for the beginning of a new sentence. This will make an endless chain that, like Tennyson's brook and, I regret to say, with as little purpose as Tennyson's brook, will run on forever. Let us see how it works in practice. Let us imagine that a speaker talking on Business Success, finds himself in a blind mental alley after having said: "The average employee does not get ahead because he takes so little real interest in his work, displays so little initiative."

"Initiative." Start a sentence with *"initiative."* You will probably have no idea of what you are going to say or how you are going to end the sentence, but, nevertheless, begin. Even a poor showing is more to be desired than utter defeat.

> Initiative means originality, doing a thing on your own, without eternally waiting to be told.

That is not a scintillating observation. It won't make speech history. But isn't it better than an agonizing silence? Our last phrase was what?—"waiting to be told." All right, let us start a new sentence with that idea.

> The constant telling and guiding and driving of employees who refuse to do any original thinking is one of the most exasperating things imaginable.

Well, we got through that one. Let us plunge again. This time we must say something about imagination:

> Imagination—that is what is needed. Vision. "Where there is no vision," Solomon said, "the people perish."

We did two that time without a hitch. Let us take heart and continue:

> The number of employees who perish each year in the battle of business is really lamentable. I say lamentable, because with just a little more loyalty, a little more ambition, a little more enthusiasm, these same men and women might have lifted themselves over the line of demarcation between success and failure. Yet the failure of business never admits that this is the case.

And so on. . . . While the speaker is saying these platitudes off the top of his mind, he should, at the same time, be thinking hard of the next point in his planned speech, of the thing he had originally intended to say. This endless chain method of thinking will, if continued very long, trap the speaker into discussing plum pudding or the price of canary birds. However, it is a splendid first aid to the injured mind broken down temporarily through forgetfullness: and, as such, it has been the means of resuscitating many a gasping and dying speech.

We Cannot Improve Our Memories for All Classes of Things

I have pointed out in this chapter how we may improve our *methods* of getting vivid impressions, of repeating and of tying our facts together. But memory is so essentially a matter of association that "there can be," as Professor James points out, "no improvement of the general or elementary faculty of memory; there can only be improvement of our memory for special systems of associated things."

By memorizing, for instance, a quotation a day from Shakespeare, we may improve our memory for literary quotations to a surprising degree. Each additional quotation will find many friends in the mind to tie to. But the memorizing of everything from Hamlet to Romeo will not necessarily aid one in retaining facts about the cotton market or the Bessemer process for desiliconizing pig iron.

Let us repeat: if we apply and use the principles discussed in this chapter, we will improve our *manner* and *efficiency* for memorizing anything; but, if we do not apply these principles, then the memorizing of ten million facts about baseball will not help us in the slightest in memorizing facts about the stock market. Such unrelated data cannot be tied together. "Our mind is essentially an associating machine."

Summary

1. "The average man," said the noted psychologist, Professor Carl Seashore, "does not use above ten per cent of his actual inherited capacity for memory. He wastes the ninety per cent by violating the natural laws of remembering."

2. These "natural laws of remembering" are three: *impression, repetition, association.*

3. Get a deep, vivid impression of the thing you wish to remember. To do that you must—

a. Concentrate. That was the secret of Theodore Roosevelt's memory.

b. Observe closely. Get an accurate impression. A camera won't take pictures in a fog; neither will your mind retain foggy impressions.

c. Get your impressions through as many of the senses as possible. Lincoln read aloud whatever he wished to remember so that he would get both a visual and an auditory impresion.

d. Above all else, be sure to get eye impressions. They stick. The nerves leading from the eye to the brain are twenty-five times as large as those leading from the ear to the brain. Mark Twain could not remember the outline of his speech when he used notes; but when he threw away his notes and used pictures to recall his various headings, all his troubles vanished.

4. The second law of memory is repetition. Thousands of Mohammedan students memorize the Koran—a book about as long as the New Testament—and they do it very largely through the power of repetition. We can memorize

anything within reason if we repeat it often enough. But bear these facts in mind as you repeat:

a. Do not sit down and repeat a thing over and over until you have it engraved on your memory. Go over it once or twice, then drop it; come back later and go over it again. Repeating at intervals, in that manner, will enable you to memorize a thing in about one-half the time required to do it at one sitting.

b. After we memorize a thing, we forget as much during the first eight hours as we do during the next thirty days; so go over your notes just a few minutes before you rise to make your talk.

5. The third law of memory is association. The only way anything can possibly be remembered at all is by associating it with some other fact. "Whatever appears in the mind," said Professor James, "must be introduced; and, when introduced, it is as the associate of something already there. . . . The one who thinks over his experiences most, and weaves them into the most synthetic relation with each other, will be the one with the best memory."

6. When you wish to associate one fact with others already in the mind, think over the new fact from all angles. Ask about it such questions as these: "Why is this so? How is this so? When is it so? Where is it so? Who said it is so?"

7. To remember a stranger's name, ask questions about it—how is it spelled, and so on? Observe his looks sharply. Try to connect the name with his face. Find out his business and try to invent some nonsense phrase that will connect his name with his business, such as was done in the Penn Athletic Club group.

8. To remember dates, associate them with prominent dates already in the mind. For example, the three hun-

dredth anniversary of Shakespeare's birth occurred during the Civil War.

9. To remember the points of your address, arrange them in such logical order that one leads naturally to the next. In addition, one can make a nonsense sentence out of the main points—for example, "The cow smoked a cigar and hooked Napoleon, and the house burned down with religion."

10. If, in spite of all precautions, you suddenly forget what you intended to say, you may be able to save yourself from complete defeat by using the last words of your last sentence as the first words in a new one. This can be continued until you are able to think of your next point.

CHAPTER FIVE

Essential Elements in Successful Speaking

The day these lines are written, January 5th, is the anniversary of the death of Sir Ernest Shackleton. He died while steaming southward on the good ship "Quest" to explore the Antarctic. The first thing that attracted one's eyes on going aboard the "Quest" were these lines engraved on a brass plate:

If you can dream and not make dreams your master;
If you can think and not make thoughts your aim;
If you can meet with triumph and disaster;
And treat those two impostors just the same,

If you can force your heart, and nerve, and sinew
To serve your turn long after they are gone;
And so hold on when there is nothing in you
Except the will which says to them, "Hold on,"

If you can fill the unforgiving minute
With sixty seconds' worth of distance run,
Yours is the earth and everything that's in it,
And, what is more, you'll be a man, my son.

"The Spirit of the Quest," Shackleton called those verses; and truly, they are the proper spirit with which a man should start out to reach the South Pole or to gain confidence in public speaking.

But that is not the spirit, I regret to add, in which all persons begin the study of public speaking. Years ago, when I first engaged in educational work, I was astounded to learn how large a percentage of students who enrolled in night schools of all sorts grew weary and fainted by the wayside before their goals were attained. The number is both lamentable and amazing. It is a sad commentary on human nature.

This is nearing the middle of the book, and I know from experience that some who are reading are already growing disheartened because they have not conquered their fear of audiences and gained self-confidence. What a pity, for "how poor are they that have not patience. What wound did ever heal but by degrees?"

The Necessity of Persistence

When we start to learn any new thing, like French, or golf, or public speaking, we never advance steadily. We do not improve gradually. We do it by sudden jerks, by abrupt starts. Then we remain stationary a time, or we may even slip back and lose some of the ground we have previously gained. These periods of stagnation, or retrogression, are well known by all psychologists; and they have been named "plateaus in the curve of learning." Students of public speaking will sometimes be stalled for weeks on one of these plateaus. Work as hard as they may, they cannot get off it. The weak ones give up in despair. Those with grit persist, and they find that suddenly, overnight, without their knowing how or why it has happened, they have made great progress. They have lifted from the plateau like an aeroplane. Abruptly they have gotten the knack of the thing. Abruptly they have acquired naturalness and force and confidence in their speaking.

You may always, as we have noted elsewhere in these

pages, experience some fleeting fear, some shock, some nervous anxiety the first few moments you face an audience. But if you will but persevere, you will soon eradicate everything but this initial fear; and that will be initial fear, and nothing more. After the first few sentences, you will have control of yourself. You will be speaking with positive pleasure.

Keeping Everlastingly at It

One time a young man who aspired to study law, wrote to Lincoln for advice, and Lincoln replied: "If you are resolutely determined to make a lawyer of yourself, the thing is more than half done already. . . . Always bear in mind that your own resolution to succeed is more important than any other one thing."

Lincoln knew. He had gone through it all. He had never, in his entire life, had more than a total of one year's schooling. And books? Lincoln once said he had walked to borrow every book within fifty miles of his home. A log fire was usually kept going all night in the cabin. Sometimes he read by the light of that fire. There were cracks between the logs, and Lincoln often kept a book sticking in a crack. As soon as it was light enough to read in the morning, he rolled over on his bed of leaves, rubbed his eyes, pulled out the book and began devouring it.

He walked twenty and thirty miles to hear a speaker and, returning home, he practiced his talks everywhere—in the fields, in the woods, before the crowds gathered at Jones' grocery at Gentryville. He joined literary and debating societies in New Salem and Springfield, and practiced speaking on the topics of the day much as you are doing now.

A sense of inferiority always troubled him. In the presence of women he was shy and dumb. When he courted Mary Todd he used to sit in the parlor, bashful and silent, unable to find words, listening while she did the talking. Yet that was the man who, by practice and home study, made himself into the speaker who debated with the accomplished orator, Senator Douglas. That was the man who, at Gettysburg, and again in his second inaugural address, rose to heights of eloquence that have rarely been attained in all the annals of mankind.

Small wonder that in view of his own terrific handicaps and pitiful struggle, he wrote: "If you are resolutely determined to make a lawyer of yourself, the thing is more than half done already."

There was an excellent picture of Abraham Lincoln in the President's office. "Often when I had some matter to decide," said Theodore Roosevelt, "something involved and difficult to dispose of, something where there were conflicting rights and interests, I would look up at Lincoln, try to imagine him in my place, try to figure out what he would do in the same circumstances. It may sound odd to you, but, frankly, it seemed to make my troubles easier of solution."

Why not try Roosevelt's plan? Why not, if you are discouraged and feeling like giving up the fight to make a speaker of yourself, why not pull out of your pocket one of the five-dollar bills that bear a likeness of Lincoln, and ask yourself what he would do under the circumstances. You know what he would do. You know what he did do. After he had been beaten by Stephen A. Douglas in the race for the U.S. Senate, he admonished his followers not to "give up after one nor one hundred defeats."

The Certainty of Reward

How I wish I could get you to prop this book open on your breakfast table every morning for a week until you had memorized these words from Professor William James, the famous Harvard psychologist:

> Let no youth have any anxiety about the upshot of his education, whatever the line of it may be. If he keeps faithfully busy each hour of the working day, he may safely leave the final result to itself. He can, with perfect certainty, count on waking up some fine morning to find

himself one of the competent ones of his generation, in whatever pursuit he may have singled out.

And now, with the renowned Professor James to fall back upon, I shall go so far as to say that if you pursue this self-study in speech faithfully and with enthusiasm, and keep right on practicing intelligently, you may confidently hope to wake up one fine morning and find yourself one of the competent speakers of your city or community.

Regardless of how fantastic that may sound to you now, *it is true as a general principle.* Exceptions, of course, there are. A man with an inferior mentality and personality, and with nothing to talk about, is not going to develop into a local Daniel Webster; but, *within reason,* the assertion is correct.

Let me illustrate by a concrete example:

Former Governor Stokes of New Jersey attended the closing banquet of a public speaking class at Trenton. He remarked that the talks he had heard the students make that evening were as good as the speeches he had heard in the House of Representatives and Senate at Washington. Those Trenton speeches were made by business men who had been tongue-tied with audience-fear a few months previously. They were not incipient Ciceros, those New Jersey business men; they were typical of the business men one finds in any American city. Yet they woke up one fine morning to find themselves among the able speakers of their city.

The entire question of your success as a speaker hinges upon only two things—your native ability, and the depth and strength of your desires. "In almost any subject," said Professor James, "your passion for the subject will save you. If you only care enough for a result, you will most certainly attain it. If you wish to be rich, you will be rich; if you wish to be learned, you will be learned; if you wish to be good, you will be good. Only you must, then, *really* wish these things and wish them with exclusiveness, and not wish at the same time a hundred other incompatible things just as strongly." And Professor James might have added, with equal truth, "If you want to be a confident public speaker, you will be a confident public speaker. But you must *really* wish it."

I have known and carefully watched literally thousands of men and women trying to gain self-confidence and the ability to talk in public. Those who succeeded were, in only a few instances, people of unusual brilliancy. For the most part, they were the ordinary run of citizens that you will find in your own home town. But they kept on. Smarter men sometimes got discouraged or too deeply immersed in money making, and they did not get very far; but the ordinary individual with grit and singleness of purpose—at the end of the chapter, he was at the top.

That is only human and natural. Don't you see the same thing occurring all the time in commerce and the professions? The elder Rockefeller said that the first essential for success in business was patience. It is likewise one of the first essentials for success here.

Marshal Foch led to victory one of the greatest armies the world has ever seen, and he declared that he had only one virtue: never despairing.

When the French had retreated to the Marne in 1914, General Joffre instructed the generals under him in charge of two million men to stop retreating and begin an offensive. This new battle, one of the most decisive in the world's history, had raged for two days when General Foch, in command of Joffre's center, sent him one of the most impressive messages in military records: "My center gives way. My right recedes. The situation is excellent. I shall attack."

That attack saved Paris.

So, when the fight seems hardest and most hopeless, when your center gives way and your right recedes, "the situation is excellent." Attack! Attack! Attack, and you will save the best part of your self—your courage and faith.

Climbing the "Wild Kaiser"

A number of summers ago, I started out to scale a peak in the Austrian Alps called the *Wilder Kaiser.* Baedeker said that the ascent was difficult, and a guide was essential for amateur climbers. We, a friend and I, had none, and we were certainly amateurs; so a third party asked us if we thought we were going to succeed. "Of course," we replied.

"What makes you think so?" he inquired.

"Others have done it without guides," I said, "so I know it is within reason, and I *never undertake anything thinking defeat.*"

As an Alpinist, I am the merest, bungling novice; but that is the proper psychology for anything from essaying public speaking to an assault on Mount Everest.

Think success. See yourself in your imagination talking in public with perfect self-control.

It is easily in your power to do this. Believe that you will succeed. Believe it firmly and you will then do what is necessary to bring success about.

Admiral Dupont gave half a dozen excellent reasons why he had not taken his gunboats into Charleston harbor. Admiral Farragut listened intently to the recital. "But there was another reason that you have not mentioned," he replied.

"What is that?" questioned Admiral Dupont.

The answer came: "You did not believe you could do it."

The most valuable thing that most members acquire from training in public speaking is an increased confidence in themselves, an additional faith in their ability to achieve. And than that, what is more important for one's success in almost any undertaking?

The Will to Win

Here is a bit of sage advice from the late Elbert Hubbard that I cannot refrain from quoting. If the average man or woman would only apply and live the wisdom contained in it, he or she would be happier, more prosperous:

> Whenever you go out of doors, draw the chin in, carry the crown of the head high and fill the lungs to the utmost; drink in the sunshine; greet your friends with a smile and put soul into every handclasp. Do not fear being misunderstood and do not waste a minute thinking about your enemies. Try to fix firmly in your mind what you would like to do, and then, without veering of direction, you will move straight to the goal. Keep your mind on the great and splendid things you would like to do, and then, as the days go gliding by, you will find yourself unconsciously seizing upon the opportunities that are required for the fulfilment of your desire, just as the coral insect takes from the running tide the elements it needs. Picture in your mind the able, earnest, useful person you desire to be, and the thought you hold is hourly transforming you into that particular individual. . . . Thought is supreme. Preserve a right mental attitude—the attitude of courage, frankness and good cheer. To think rightly is to create. All things come through desire and every sincere prayer is answered. We become like that on which our hearts are fixed. Carry your chin in and the crown of your head high. We are gods in the chrysalis.

Napoleon, Wellington, Lee, Grant, Foch—all great military leaders have recognized that an army's will to win and its confidence in its ability to win, do more than any other one thing to determine its success.

"Ninety thousand conquered men," said Marshall Foch, "retire before ninety thousand conquering men only because they have had enough, because they no longer believe in victory, because they are demoralized—at the end of their moral resistance."

In other words, the ninety thousand retiring men are not really whipped physically; but they are conquered because they are whipped mentally, because they have lost their courage and confidence. There is no hope for an army like that. There is no hope for a man like that.

Chaplain Frazier, a former ranking chaplain of the U.S. Navy, interviewed those who wished to enlist for the chaplaincy service during the First World War. When asked what qualities were essential for the success of a navy chaplain, he replied with four G'*s*: "Grace, gumption, grit, and *guts.*"

Those are also the requisites for success in speaking. Take them as your motto. Take this Robert Service poem as your battle song:

When you're lost in the wild, and you're scared as a child,
And death looks you bang in the eye.
And you're sore as a boil, it's according to Hoyle
To cock your revolver and . . . die.
But the code of a man, says: "Fight all you can,"
And self-dissolution is barred.
In hunger and woe, oh, it's easy to blow . . .
It's the hell-served-for-breakfast that's hard.

You're sick of the game! "Well, now, that's a shame."
You're young and you're brave and you're bright.
"You've had a raw deal!" I know—but don't squeal.
Buck up, do your damnedest, and fight.
It's the plugging away that will win you the day,
So don't be a piker, old pard!
Just draw on your grit; it's so easy to quit:
It's the keeping-your-chin-up that's hard.

It's easy to cry that you're beaten—and die.
It's easy to crawfish and crawl;
But to fight and to fight when hope's out of sight,
Why, that's the best game of them all!

And though you come out of each gruelling bout
All broken and beaten and scarred,
Just have one more try—it's dead easy to die,
It's the keeping-on-living that's hard.

Summary

1. We never learn anything—be it golf, French, or public speaking—by means of gradual improvement. We advance by sudden jerks and abrupt starts. Then we may remain stationary for a few weeks, or even lose some of the proficiency we have gained. Psychologists call these periods of stagnation "plateaus in the curve of learning." We may strive hard for a long time and not be able to get off one of these "plateaus" and onto an upward ascent again. Some people, not realizing this curious fact about the way we progress, get discouraged on these plateaus and abandon all effort. That is extremely regrettable, for if they were to persist, if they were to keep on practicing, they would suddenly find that they had lifted like an aeroplane and made tremendous progress again overnight.

2. You may never be able to speak without some nervous anxiety just before you begin. But, if you will persevere, you will soon eradicate everything but this initial fear; and, after you have spoken for a few seconds, that too will disappear.

3. Professor James has pointed out that one need have no anxiety about the upshot of his education, that if he keeps faithfully busy, "he can, with perfect certainty, count on waking up some fine morning to find himself one of the competent ones of his generation, in whatever pursuit he may have singled out." This psychological truth that the famous sage of Harvard has enunciated, applies to you and your efforts in learning to speak. There can be no question about that. The men who have succeeded in this have not been, as a general rule, men of extraordinary ability. But they were endowed with persistence and dogged determination. They kept on. They arrived.

4. Think success in your public speaking work. You will then do the things necessary to bring success about.

5. If you get discouraged, try Teddy Roosevelt's plan of looking at Lincoln's picture and asking yourself what he would have done under similar circumstances.

6. The ranking chaplain of the U.S. Navy during the First World War said that the qualities essential for the success of a chaplain in the service could be enumerated with four words commencing with G. What are they?

CHAPTER SIX

The Secret of Good Delivery

Shortly after the close of the First World War, I met two brothers in London, Sir Ross and Sir Keith Smith. They had just made the first aeroplane flight from London to Australia, had won the fifty thousand dollar prize offered by the Australian government, had created a sensation throughout the British Empire, and had been knighted by the King.

Captain Hurley, a well-known scenic photographer, had flown with them over a part of their trip, taking motion pictures; so I helped them prepare an illustrated travel talk of their flight and trained them in the delivery of it. They gave it twice daily for four months in Philharmonic Hall, London, one speaking in the afternoon and the other at night.

They had had identically the same experience, had sat side by side as they flew halfway around the world; and they delivered the same talk, almost word for word. Yet, somehow it didn't sound like the same talk at all.

There is something besides the mere words in a talk which counts. It is the flavor with which they are delivered. "It is not so much what you say as how you say it."

I once sat beside a young woman at a public concert

who was reading, as Paderewski played them, the notes of a Mazurka by Chopin. She was mystified. She couldn't understand. His fingers were touching precisely the same notes that hers had touched when she had played it; yet her rendition had been commonplace, and his was inspired, a thing of surpassing beauty, a performance that held the audience enthralled. It was not the mere notes that he touched; it was the way he touched them, a feeling, an artistry, a personality that he put into the touching that made all the difference between mediocrity and genius.

Brullof, the great Russian painter, once corrected a pupil's study. The pupil looked in amazement at the altered drawing, exclaiming: "Why, you have touched it only a tiny bit, but it is quite another thing." Brullof replied: "Art begins where the tiny bit begins." That is as true of speaking as it is of painting and of Paderewski's playing.

The same thing holds true when one is touching words. There is an old saying in the English Parliament that everything depends upon the manner in which one speaks and not upon the matter. Quintilian said that long ago when England was one of the outlying colonies of Rome.

Like most old sayings, it needs to be taken *cum grano salis;* but good delivery will make very thin matter go a very long way. I have often noticed in college contests that it is not always the speaker with the best material who wins. Rather, it is the speaker who can talk so well that his material sounds best.

"Three things matter in a speech," Lord Morley once observed with gay cynicism, "who says it, how he says it, and what he says—and, of the three, the last matters the least." An exaggeration? Yes, but scratch the surface of it and you will find the truth shining through.

Edmund Burke wrote speeches so excellent in logic and reasoning and composition that they are today studied as classic models of oration in half the colleges of the land; yet Burke, as a speaker, was a notorious failure. He didn't have the ability to deliver his gems, to make them interesting and forceful; so he was called "the dinner bell" of the House of Commons. When he arose to talk, the other members coughed and shuffled and went out in droves.

You can throw a steel-jacketed bullet at a man with all your might, and you cannot make even a dent in his clothing. But put powder behind a tallow candle and you can shoot it through a pine board. Many a tallow-candle speech with powder makes, I regret to say, more of an impression than a steel-jacketed talk with no force behind it.

Look well, therefore, to your delivery.

What Is Delivery?

What does a department store do when it "delivers" the article you have bought? Does the driver just toss the package into the backyard and let it go at that? Is merely getting a thing out of one's own hands the same as getting it delivered? The messenger boy with a telegram delivers the "wire" into the direct possession of the person for whom it is intended. But do all speakers?

Let me give you an illustration that is typical of the fashion in which thousands of people talk. I happened on one occasion to be stopping in Mürren, a summer resort in the Swiss Alps. I was living at a hotel operated by a London company; and they usually sent out from England a couple of lecturers each week to talk to the guests. One of them was a well-known English novelist. Her topic was "The Future of the Novel." She admitted that she had not selected the subject herself; and, the long and short of it was that she had nothing to say about it that she really cared enough about saying to make it worth while expressing. She had hurriedly made some rambling notes; and she stood before the audience, ignoring her hearers, not even looking at them, staring sometimes over their heads, sometimes at her notes, sometimes at the floor. She called off her words into the primeval void with a far-away look in her eyes and a far-away ring in her voice.

That kind of performance isn't delivering a talk at all. It is a soliloquy. It has no sense of communication. And that is the first essential of good talking: *a sense of com-*

munication. The audience must feel that there is a message being delivered straight from the mind and heart of the speaker to their minds and their hearts. The kind of talk I have just described might just as well have been spoken out in the sandy, waterless wastes of the Gobi Desert. In fact, it sounded as if it were being delivered in some such spot rather than to a group of living human beings.

This matter of delivering a talk is, at the same time, a very simple and a very intricate process. It is also a very much misunderstood and abused one.

The Secret of Good Delivery

An enormous amount of nonsense and twaddle has been written about delivery. It has been shrouded in rules and rites and made mysterious. Old-fashioned "elocution," that abomination in the sight of God and man, has often made it ridiculous. The business man, going to the library or bookshop has found volumes on "oratory" that were utterly useless. In spite of progress in other directions, some schoolboys are still being forced to recite the ornate "oratory" of Webster and Ingersoll—a thing that is as much out of style and as far removed from the spirit of this age as the hats worn by Mrs. Ingersoll and Mrs. Webster would be if they were resurrected today.

An entirely new school of speaking has sprung up since the Civil War. In keeping with the spirit of the times, it is as direct as a telegram. The verbal fireworks that were once the vogue would no longer be tolerated by an audience in this year of grace.

A modern audience, regardless of whether it is fifteen people at a business conference or a thousand people under a tent, wants the speaker to talk just as directly as he would in a chat, and in the same general manner that he would employ in speaking to one of them in conversation.

In the same *manner,* but not with the same amount of force. If he tries that, he will hardly be heard. In order to appear natural he has to use much more energy in talking to forty people than he does in talking to one; just as a statue on top of a building has to be of heroic size in order to make it appear of lifelike proportions to an observer on the ground.

At the close of Mark Twain's lecture in a Nevada mining camp, an old prospector approached him and inquired: "Be them your natural tones of eloquence?"

That is what the audience wants: "your natural tones of eloquence," enlarged a bit.

Speak to the Community Chest just as you would to John Henry Smith. What is a meeting of the Chest Committee after all, but a mere collection of John Henry Smiths? Won't the same methods that are successful with those men and women individually be successful with them collectively?

I have just described the delivery of a certain novelist. In the same ballroom in which she had spoken, I had the pleasure, a few nights later, of hearing Sir Oliver Lodge. His subject was "Atoms and Worlds." He devoted to it more than half a century of thought and study and experiment and investigation. He had something that was essentially a part of his heart and mind and life, something that he wanted very much to say. He forgot—and I, for one, thanked God that he did forget—that he was trying to make a speech. That was the least of his worries. He was concerned only with telling the audience about atoms, telling us accurately and lucidly and feelingly. He was earnestly trying to get us to see what he saw and to feel what he felt.

And what was the result? He delivered a remarkable talk. It had both charm and power. It made a deep impression. He was a speaker of unusual ability. Yet I am sure he didn't regard himself in that light. I am sure that few people who heard him ever think of him as a public speaker at all.

If you who read this book speak in public so that people hearing you will suspect that you have had training in public speaking, you will not be a credit to the author. He would desire you to speak with such intensified and exalted naturalness that your auditors would never dream that you had been trained. A good window does not call attention to itself. It merely lets in the light. A good speaker is like that. He is so natural that his hearers never notice his manner of speaking; they are conscious only of his matter.

Henry Ford's Advice

"All Fords are exactly alike," their maker used to say, "but no two men are just alike. Every new life is a new thing under the sun; there has never been anything just like it before, and never will be again. A young man ought to get that idea about himself; he should look for the single spark of individuality that makes him different from other folks, and develop that for all he is worth. Society and schools may try to iron it out of him; their tendency is to put us all in the same mold, but I say don't let that spark be lost; it's your only real claim to importance."

All that is doubly true of public speaking. There is no other human being in the world like you. Hundreds of millions of people have two eyes and a nose and a mouth; but none of them look precisely like you; and none of them have exactly your traits and methods and cast of mind. Few of them will talk and express themselves just as you do when you are speaking naturally. In other words, you have an individuality. As a speaker, it is your most precious possession. Cling to it. Cherish it. Develop it. It is the spark that will put force and sincerity into your speaking. "It is your only real claim to importance."

Sir Oliver Lodge spoke differently from other men, because he himself was different. The man's manner of speaking was as essentially a part of his own individuality as were his beard and bald head. If he had tried to imitate Lloyd George, he would have been false, he would have failed.

The most famous debates ever held in America took place in 1858 in the prairie towns of Illinois between Senator Stephen A. Douglas and Abraham Lincoln. Lincoln was tall and awkward. Douglas was short and graceful. These men were as unlike in their characters and mentality and personalities and dispositions as they were in their physiques.

Douglas was the cultured man of the world. Lincoln was the rail splitter who went to the front door in his sock feet to receive company. Douglas' gestures were graceful. Lincoln's were ungainly. Douglas was utterly destitute of humor. Lincoln was one of the greatest storytellers who ever lived. Douglas seldom used a smile. Lincoln constantly argued by analogy and illustration. Douglas was haughty and overbearing. Lincoln was humble and forgiving. Douglas thought in quick flashes. Lincoln's mental processes were much slower. Douglas spoke with the impetuous rush of a whirlwind. Lincoln was quieter and deeper and more deliberate.

Both of these men, unlike as they were, were able speakers because they had the courage and good sense to be themselves. If either had tried to imitate the other, he would have failed miserably. But each one, by using to the utmost his own peculiar talents, made himself individual and powerful. *Go thou and do likewise.*

That is an easy direction to give. But is it an easy one to follow? Most emphatically it is not. As Marshal Foch said of the art of war: "It is simple in its conception, but unfortunately complicated in its execution."

It takes practice to be natural before an audience. Actors know that. When you were a little boy or girl, four years old, you probably could, had you but tried, have mounted a platform and "recited" naturally to an audience. But when you are twenty-and-four, or forty-and-four, what will happen if you mount a platform and start to speak? Will you retain that unconscious naturalness that you possessed at four? You may, but it is dollars to doughnuts that you will become stiff and stilted and mechanical, and draw back into your shell like a snapping turtle.

The problem of teaching or of training people in delivery is not one of superimposing additional characteristics; it is largely one of removing impediments, of freeing them, of getting them to speak with the same naturalness that they would display if someone were to knock them down.

Hundreds of times I have stopped speakers in the midst of their talks and implored them to "talk like a human being." Hundreds of nights I have come home mentally fatigued and nervously exhausted from trying to drill and force people to talk naturally. No, believe me, it is not so easy as it sounds.

And the only way under high heaven by which you can get the knack of this enlarged naturalness is by practice. And, as you practice, if you find yourself talking in a stilted manner, pause and say sharply to yourself mentally: "Here! What is wrong? Wake up. Be human." Then pick out someone in the audience, some person in the back, the dullest looking character you can find, and talk to him or her. Forget there is anyone else present at all. *Converse* with him. Imagine that he has asked you a question and that you are answering it. If he were to stand up and talk to you, and you were to talk back to him, that process would immediately and inevitably make your talking more conversational, more natural, more direct. So, imagine that that is precisely what is taking place.

You may go so far as actually to ask questions and answer them. For example, in the midst of your talk, you may say, "and you ask what proof have I for this assertion? I have adequate proof and here it is . . ." Then proceed to answer the imaginary question. That sort of thing can be done very naturally. It will break up the monotony of one's delivery; it will make it direct and pleasant and conversational.

Sincerity and enthusiasm and high earnestness will help you, too. When a person is under the influence of his feelings, his real self comes to the surface. The bars are down. The heat of his emotions has burned all barriers away. He acts spontaneously. He talks spontaneously. He is natural.

So, in the end, even this matter of delivery comes back to the thing which has already been emphasized repeatedly in these pages: namely, put your heart in your talks.

"I shall never forget," said Dean Brown in his lectures on Preaching before the Yale Divinity School, "the description given by a friend of mine of a service which he once attended in the city of London. The preacher was George

MacDonald. He read for the Scripture lesson that morning the eleventh chapter of Hebrews. When the time came for the sermon, he said: 'You have all heard about these men of faith. I shall not try to tell you what faith is. There are theological professors who could do that much better than I could do it. I am here to help you believe.' Then followed such a simple, heartfelt and majestic manifestation of the man's own faith in those unseen realities which are eternal, as to beget faith in the minds and hearts of all his hearers. *His heart was in his work, and his delivery was effective because it rested back upon the genuine beauty of his own inner life.*"

"His heart was in his work." That is the secret. Yet I know that advice like this is not popular. It seems vague. It sounds indefinite. The average student wants foolproof rules. Something definite. Something he can put his hands on. Rules as precise as the directions for operating a car.

That is what he wants. That is what I would like to give him. It would be easy for him. It would be easy for me. There are such rules, and there is only one little thing wrong with them: they don't work. They take all the naturalness and spontaneity and life and juice out of speaking. I know. In my younger days I wasted a great deal of energy trying them. They won't appear in these pages for, as Josh Billings observed in one of his lighter moments: "There ain't no use in knowin' so many things that ain't so."

Do You Do These Things When You Talk in Public?

We are going to discuss here some of the features of natural speaking in order to make them more clear, more vivid. I have hesitated about doing it, for someone is almost sure to say: "Ah, I see, just force myself to do these things and I'll be all right." No, you won't. *Force* yourself to do them and you will be all wooden and all mechanical.

You used most of these principles yesterday in your conversation, used them as unconsciously as you digested your dinner last night. That is the way to use them. It is the *only* way. And it will come, as far as public speaking is concerned, as we have already said, only by practice.

First: Stress Important Words, Subordinate Unimportant Ones

In conversation, we hit one syllable in a word, and hit it hard, and hurry over the others like a pay car passing a string of hoboes; e.g., MassaCHUsetts, afFLICtion, atTRACtiveness, enVIRonment. We do almost the samething with a sentence. We make one or two important words tower up like the Empire State Building on Fifth Avenue, New York.

This is not a strange or unusual process I am describing. Listen. You can hear it going on about you all the time. You yourself did it a hundred, maybe a thousand, times yesterday. You will doubtlessly do it a hundred times tomorrow.

Here is an example. Read the following quotation, striking the words in big type hard. Run over the others quickly. What is the effect?

> I have SUCCEEDED in whatever I have undertaken, because I have WILLED it. I have NEVER HESITATED which has given me an ADVANTAGE over the rest of mankind.—Napoleon.

This is not the only way to read these lines. Another speaker would do it differently perhaps. There are no ironclad rules for emphasis. It all depends.

Read these selections aloud in an earnest manner, trying to make the ideas clear and convincing. Don't you find yourself stressing the big, important words and hurrying over the others?

> If you think you are beaten, you are.
> If you think you dare not, you don't.
> If you'd like to win, but think you can't,
> It's almost a cinch you won't.

Life's battles don't always go
To the stronger or faster man;
But soon or late the man who wins
Is the one who thinks he can.
—Anon.

Perhaps there is no more important component of character than steadfast resolution. The boy who is going to make a great man, or is going to count in any way in afterlife, must make up in his mind not merely to overcome a thousand obstacles, but to win in spite of a thousand repulses and defeats.
—Theodore Roosevelt.

Second: Change Your Pitch

The pitch of our voices in conversation flows up and down the scale from high to low and back again, never resting, but always shifting like the face of the sea. Why? No one knows, and no one cares. The effect is pleasing, and it is the way of nature. We never had to learn to do this: it came to us as children, unsought and unaware, but let us stand up and face an audience, and the chances are our voices will become as dull, flat and monotonous as the alkali deserts of Nevada.

When you find yourself talking in a monotonous pitch—and usually it will be a high one—just pause for a second and say to yourself: "I am speaking like a wooden Indian. *Talk* to these people. Be human. Be natural."

Will that kind of lecture to yourself help you any? A little, perhaps. The pause itself will help you. You have to work out your own salvation by practice.

You can make any phrase or word that you choose stand out like a green bay tree in the front yard by either suddenly lowering or raising your pitch on it. Dr. S. Parkes Cadman, the famous Congregational minister of Brooklyn, often did it. So did Sir Oliver Lodge. So did Bryan. So did Roosevelt. So does almost every speaker of note.

In the following quotations, try saying the italicized

words in a much lower pitch than you use for the rest of the sentence. What is the effect?

> I have but one merit, that of *never despairing.*—Marshal Foch.

> The great aim of education is not knowledge, *but action.*—Herbert Spencer.

> I have lived eighty-six years. I have watched men climb up to success, hundreds of them, and of all the elements that are important for success, *the most important is faith.*—Cardinal Gibbons.

Third: Vary Your Rate of Speaking

When a little child talks, or when we talk in ordinary conversation, we *constantly change our rate of speaking.* It is pleasing. It is natural. It is unconscious. It is emphatic. It is, in fact, one of the very best of all possible ways to make an idea stand out prominently.

Walter B. Stevens, in his *Reporter's Lincoln,* issued by the Missouri Historical Society, tells us that this was one of Lincoln's favorite methods of driving a point home:

> He would speak several words with great rapidity, come to the word or phrase he wished to emphasize, and let his voice linger and bear hard on that, and then he would rush to the end of his sentence like lightning. . . . He would devote as much time to the word or two he wished to emphasize as he did to half a dozen less important words following it.

Such a method invariably arrests attention. To illustrate: I have often quoted in a public talk the following statement by Cardinal Gibbons. I wanted to emphasize the idea of courage; so I lingered on these italicized words, drew them out and spoke as if I, myself, were impressed with them—and I was. Will you please read the selection aloud, trying the same method and note the results.

> A short time before his death, Cardinal Gibbons said: "I have lived *eighty-six years.* I have watched men *climb* up to *success, hundreds* of them, and of all the elements that are *important* for success, the *most important* is *faith. No great thing comes to any man unless he has courage.*"

Try this: say "thirty million dollars" quickly and with an air of triviality so that it sounds like a very small sum. Now, say "thirty thousand dollars"; say it slowly; say it feelingly; say it as if you were tremendously impressed with the hugeness of the amount. Haven't you now made the thirty thousand sound larger than the thirty million?

Fourth: Pause Before and After Important Ideas

Lincoln often paused in his speaking. When he had come to a big idea that he wished to impress deeply on the minds of his hearers, he bent forward, looked directly into their eyes for a moment and said nothing at all. This sudden silence had the same effect as a sudden noise: it attracted notice. It made everyone attentive, alert, awake to what was coming next. For example, when his famous debates with Douglas were drawing to a close, when all the indications pointed to his defeat, he became depressed, his old habitual melancholy stealing over him at times, and imparting to his words a touching pathos. In one of his concluding speeches, he suddenly *"stopped and stood silent for a moment,* looking around upon the throng of half-indifferent, half-friendly faces before him, with those deep-sunken weary eyes that always seemed full of unshed tears. Folding his hands, as if they too were tired of the helpless fight, he said, in his peculiar monotone: 'My friends, it makes little difference, very little difference, whether Judge Douglas or myself is elected to the United States Senate; but the great issue which we have submitted to you to-day is far above and beyond any personal interests or the political fortunes of any man. And my friends,' here he paused again, and the audience were intent on every word, 'that issue will live and breathe and burn when the poor, feeble, stammering tongues of Judge Douglas and myself are silent in the grave.' "

"These simple words," relates one of his biographers, "and the manner in which they were spoken, touched every heart to the core."

Lincoln also paused after the phrases he wanted to emphasize. He added to their force by keeping silent while the meaning sank in and effected its mission.

Sir Oliver Lodge paused frequently in his speaking, both before and after important ideas; paused as often as three or four times in one sentence, but he did it naturally and unconsciously. No man, unless he were analyzing Sir Oliver's methods, would notice it.

"By your silence," said Kipling, "ye shall speak." Nowhere is silence more golden than when it is judiciously used in talking. It is a powerful tool, too important to be ignored, yet it is usually neglected by the beginning speaker.

In the following excerpt from Holman's *Ginger Talks,* I have marked the places where a speaker might profitably pause. I do not say that these are the *only* places where one ought to pause, or even the best places. I say only that it is *one* way of doing it. Where to pause is not a matter of hard and fast rules. It is a matter of meaning and temperament and feeling. You might pause one place in a speech to-day, and in another place in the same speech to-morrow.

Read this selection aloud without pausing; then read it again, making the pauses I have indicated. What is the effect of the pauses?

> "Selling goods is a battle" (pause and let the idea of *battle* soak in) "and only fighters can win in it." (Pause and let that point soak in.) "We may not like these conditions, but we didn't have the making of them and we can't alter them." (Pause.) "Take your courage with

you when you enter the selling game." (Pause.) "If you don't," (pause and lengthen out suspense for a second) "you'll strike out every time you come to bat, and score nothing higher than a string of goose eggs." (Pause.) "No man ever made a three-base hit who was afraid of the pitcher" (pause and let your point soak in)—"remember that." (Pause and let it soak in some more.) "The fellow who knocks the cover off the ball or lifts it over the fence for a home run is always the chap who steps up to the plate" (pause and increase the suspense as to what you are going to say about this extraordinary player) "with grim determination in his heart."

Read the following quotations aloud and with force and meaning. Observe where you naturally pause.

The great American desert is not located in Idaho, New Mexico or Arizona. It is located under the hat of the average man. The great American desert is a mental desert rather than a physical desert.—J. S. Knox.

There is no panacea for human ills; the nearest approach to it is publicity.—Professor Foxwell.

There are two people I must please—God and Garfield. I must live with Garfield here, with God hereafter.—James A. Garfield.

A speaker may follow the directions I have set down in this chapter and still have a hundred faults. He may talk in public just as he does in conversation and consequently, he may speak with an unpleasant voice and make grammatical errors and be awkward and offensive and do a score of unpleasant things. A person's natural method of everyday talking may need a vast number of improvements. Perfect your natural method of talking in conversation, and then carry that method to the platform.

Summary

1. There is something besides the mere words in a talk which counts. It is the flavor with which they are delivered. "It is not so much what you say as how you say it."

2. Many speakers ignore their hearers, stare over their heads or at the floor. They seem to be delivering a soliloquy. There is no sense of communication, no give and take between the audience and the speaker. That kind of attitude would kill a conversation; it also kills a speech.

3. Good delivery is conversational tone and directness enlarged. Talk to the Community Chest just as you would to John Smith. What is the Chest Committee, after all, but a collection of John Smiths?

4. Everyone has the ability to deliver a talk. If you question this statement, try it out for yourself; knock down the most ignorant man you know; when he gets on his feet, he will probably say some things, and his manner of saying them will be almost flawless. We want you to take that same naturalness with you when you speak in public. To develop it, you must practice. Don't imitate others. If you speak spontaneously you will speak differently from anyone else in the world. Put your own individuality, your own characteristic manner into your delivery.

5. Talk to your hearers just as if you expected them to stand up in a moment and talk back to you. If they were to rise and ask you questions, your delivery would almost be sure to improve emphatically and at once. So *imagine* that someone has asked you a question, and that you are repeating it. Say aloud, "You ask how do I know this? I'll tell you." . . . That sort of thing will seem perfectly natural; it will break up the formality of your phraseology; it will warm and humanize your manner of talking.

6. Put your heart into your talking. Real emotional sincerity will help more than all the rules in Christendom.

7. Here are four things that all of us do unconsciously in earnest conversation. But do you do them when you are talking in public? Most people do not.

a. Do you stress the important words in a sentence and subordinate the unimportant ones? Do you give almost every word including *the, and, but,* approximately the same amount of attention, or do you speak a sentence in much the same way that you say MassaCHUsetts?

b. Does the pitch of your voice flow up and down the scale from high to low and back again—as the pitch of a little child does when speaking?

c. Do you vary your rate of speaking, running rapidly over the unimportant words, spending more time on the ones you wish to make stand out?

d. Do you pause before and after your important ideas?

CHAPTER SEVEN

Platform Presence and Personality

The Carnegie Institute of Technology at one time gave intelligence tests to one hundred prominent business men. The tests were similar to those used in the army during the war; and the results led the Institute to declare that personality contributes more to business success than does superior intelligence.

That is a very significant pronouncement: very significant for the business man, very significant for the educator, very significant for the professional man, very significant for the speaker.

Personality—with the exception of preparation—is probably the most important factor in public address. "In eloquent speaking," declared Elbert Hubbard, "it is manner that wins, not words." Rather it is manner plus ideas. But personality is a vague and elusive thing, defying analysis like the perfume of the violet. It is the whole combination of the person: physical, spiritual, mental; traits, predilections, tendencies, temperament, cast of mind, vigor, experience, training, the whole life. It is as complex as Einstein's theory of relativity, almost as little understood.

A personality is determined by inheritance and environment and is extremely difficult to alter or improve. Yet we can, by taking thought, strengthen it to some extent and make it more forceful, more attractive. At any rate, we can strive to get the utmost possible out of this strange thing that nature has given us. The subject is of vast importance to every one of us. The possibilities for improvement, limited as they are, are still large enough to warrant a discussion and investigation.

If you wish to make the most of your individuality, go before your audience rested. A tired speaker is not magnetic nor attractive. Don't make the all-too-common error of putting off your preparation and your planning until the very last moment, and then working at a furious pace, trying to make up for lost time. If you do, you are bound to store up bodily poisons and brain fatigues that will prove terrific drags, holding you down, sapping your vitality, weakening both your brain and your nerves.

If you must make an important talk to a committee meeting at four, have a light lunch, if possible, and the refreshment of a siesta. Rest—that is what you need, physical and mental and nervous.

Geraldine Farrar used to shock her newly made friends by saying good night and retiring early, leaving them to talk the remainder of the evening with her husband. She knew the demands of her art.

Madame Nordica said that being a prima donna meant giving up everything one liked: social affairs, friends, tempting meals.

When you have to make an important talk, beware of your hunger. Eat as sparingly as a saint. On Sunday afternoons, Henry Ward Beecher used to have crackers and milk at five, and nothing after that.

"When I am singing in the evening," said Madame Melba, "I do not dine but have a very light repast at five o'clock, consisting of either fish, chicken, or sweetbread, with a baked apple and a glass of water. I always find myself very hungry for supper when I get home from the opera or concert."

How wisely Melba and Beecher acted, I never realized

until after I became a professional speaker myself and tried to deliver a two-hour talk each evening after having consumed a hearty meal. Experience taught me that I couldn't enjoy a *filet de sole aux pommes nature* and follow that by a beefsteak and French fried potatoes and salad and vegetables and a dessert, and then stand up an hour afterward and do either myself or my subject or my body justice. The blood that ought to have been in my brain was down in my stomach wrestling with that steak and potatoes. Paderewski was right: he said when he ate what he wanted to eat before a concert, the animal in him got uppermost, that it even got into his finger tips and clogged and dulled his playing.

Why One Speaker Draws Better Than Another

Do nothing to dull your energy. It is magnetic. Vitality, aliveness, enthusiasm: they are among the first qualities I have always sought for in employing speakers and instructors of speaking. People cluster around the energetic speaker, the human dynamo of energy, like wild geese around a field of autumn wheat.

I have often seen this illustrated by the open-air speakers in Hyde Park, London. A spot near Marble Arch entrance is a rendezvous for speakers of every creed and color. On a Sunday afternoon, one can take his choice and listen to a Catholic explaining the doctrine of the infallibility of the Pope, to a Socialist propounding the economic gospel of Karl Marx, to an Indian explaining why it is right and proper for a Mohammedan to have two wives, and so on. Hundreds crowd about one speaker, while his neighbor has only a handful. Why? Is the topic always an adequate explanation of the disparity between the drawing powers of different speakers? No. More often the explanation is to be found in the speaker himself: he is more interested and, consequently, interesting. He talks with more life and spirit. He radiates vitality and animation; they always challenge attention.

How Are You Affected by Clothes?

An inquiry was sent to a large group of people by a psychologist and university president, asking them the impression clothes made on them. All but unanimously, they testified that when they were well groomed and faultlessly and immaculately attired, the knowledge of it, the feeling of it, had an effect which, while it was difficult to explain, was still very definite, very real. It gave them more confidence; brought them increased faith in themselves; heightened their self-respect. They declared that when they had the look of success they found it easier to think success, to achieve success. Such is the effect of clothes on the wearer himself.

What effect do they have on an audience? I have noticed time and again that if the speaker is a man with baggy trousers, shapeless coat and footwear, fountain pen and pencils peeping out of his breast pocket, a newspaper or a pipe and can of tobacco sticking out the sides of his garment, or is a woman with an ugly, bulging purse and with her slip showing—I have noticed that an audience has as little respect for that person as the speaker has for his or her own appearance. Aren't they very likely to assume that the mind is as sloppy as the unkempt hair, unpolished shoes, or bulging handbag?

One of the Regrets of Grant's Life

When General Lee came to Appomattox Court House to surrender his army, he was immaculately attired in a new uniform and, at his side, hung a sword of extraordinary value. Grant was coatless and swordless, and was wearing the shirt and trousers of a private. "I must have contrasted very strangely," he wrote in his Memoirs, "with a man so handsomely dressed, six feet high, and of faultless form." The fact that he had not been appropriately attired for this historic occasion came to be one of the real regrets of Grant's life.

The Department of Agriculture in Washington has several hundred stands of bees on its experimental farm. Each hive has a large magnifying glass built into it, and the interior can be flooded with electric light by pressing a button; so, any moment, night or day, these bees are liable to be subject to the minutest scrutiny. A speaker is like that: he is under the magnifying glass, he is in the spotlight, all eyes are upon him. The smallest disharmony in his personal appearance now looms up like Pike's Peak from the plains.

"Even Before We Speak, We Are Condemned or Approved"

A number of years ago I was writing for the *American Magazine* the life story of a certain New York banker. I asked one of his friends to explain the reason for his success. No small amount of it, he said, was due to the man's winning smile. At first thought, that may sound like exaggeration but I believe it is really true. Other men, scores of them, hundreds of them, may have had more experience and as good financial judgment, but he had an additional asset they didn't possess—he had a most agreeable personality. And a warm, welcoming smile was one of the striking features of it. It gained one's confidence immediately. It secured one's good will instantly. We all want to see a man like that succeed; and it is a real pleasure to give him our patronage.

"He who cannot smile," says a Chinese proverb, "ought not to keep a shop." And isn't a smile just as welcome before an audience as behind a counter? I am thinking now of a particular student who attended a course in public speaking conducted by the Brooklyn Chamber of Commerce. He always came out before the audience with an air that said he liked to be there, that he loved the job that was before him. He always smiled and acted as if he were glad to see us; and so immediately and inevitably his hearers warmed toward him and welcomed him.

But I have seen speakers who walked out in a cold, perfunctory manner as if they had a disagreeable task to perform, and would thank God when it was over. We in the audience were soon feeling the same way. These attitudes are contagious.

"Like begets like," observes Professor Overstreet in *Influencing Human Behavior*. "If we are interested in our audience, there is a likelihood that our audience will be interested in us. If we scowl at our audience, there is every likelihood that inwardly or outwardly they will scowl at us. If we are timid and rather flustered, they likewise will lack confidence in us. If we are brazen and boastful, they will react with their own self-protective egotism. Even before we speak, very often, we are condemned or approved. There is every reason, therefore, that we should make certain that our attitude is such as to elicit warm response."

Crowd Your Audience Together

As a public lecturer, I have frequently spoken to a small audience scattered through a large hall in the afternoon, and to a large audience packed into the same hall at night. The evening audience has laughed heartily at the same things that brought only a smile to the faces of the afternoon group; the evening crowd has applauded generously at the very places where the afternoon gathering was utterly unresponsive. Why?

For one thing, the elderly women and the children that are likely to come in the afternoon cannot be expected to be as demonstrative as the more vigorous and discriminating evening crowd; but that is only a partial explanation.

The fact is that no audience will be easily moved when it is scattered. Nothing so dampens enthusiasm as wide, open spaces and empty chairs between the listeners.

Henry Ward Beecher said in his Yale Lectures on Preaching:

> People often say, "Do you not think it is much more inspiring to speak to a large audience than a small one?" No, I say; I can speak just as well to twelve persons as to a thousand, provided those twelve are crowded around me and close together, so that they can touch each other. But even a thousand people with four feet of space between every two of them, would be just the same as an empty room. . . . Crowd your audience together and you will set them off with half the effort.

A man in a large audience tends to lose his individuality. He becomes a member of the crowd and is swayed far more easily than he would be as a single individual. He will laugh at and applaud things that would leave him unmoved if he were only one of half a dozen people listening to you.

It is far easier to get people to act as a body than to act singly. Men going into battle, for example, invariably want to do the most dangerous and reckless thing in the world—they want to huddle together. During the late war, German soldiers were known to go into battle at times with their arms locked about one another.

Crowds! Crowds! Crowds! They are a curious phenomenon. All great popular movements and reforms have been carried forward by the aid of the crowd mentality. An interesting book on this subject is Everett Dean Martin's *The Behavior of Crowds.*

If we are going to talk to a small group, we should choose a small room. Better to pack the aisles of a small place than to have people scattered through the lonely, deadening spaces of a large hall.

If your hearers are scattered, ask them to move down front and be seated near you. Insist on this, before you start speaking.

Unless the audience is a fairly large one, and there is a real reason, a necessity, for the speaker to stand on a platform, don't do so. Get down on the same level with them. Stand near them. Break up all formality. Get an intimate contact. Make the thing conversational.

Major Pond Smashed the Windows

Keep the air fresh. In the well-known process of public speaking, oxygen is just as essential as the larynx, pharynx and human epiglottis. All the eloquence of Cicero, and all the feminine pulchritude in the Music Hall Rockettes, could hardly keep an audience awake in a room poisoned with bad air. So, when I am one of a number of speakers, before beginning, I almost always ask the audience to stand up and rest for two minutes while the windows are thrown open.

For fourteen years Major James B. Pond traveled all over the United States and Canada as manager for Henry Ward Beecher when that famous Brooklyn preacher was at his flood tide as a popular lecturer. Before the audience assembled, Pond always visited the hall or church or theater where Beecher was to appear, and rigorously inspected the lighting, seating, temperature and ventilation. Pond had been a blustering, roaring old army officer; he loved to exercise authority; so if the place was too warm or the air was dead and he could not get the windows open, he hurled books through them, smashing and shattering the glass. He believed with Spurgeon that "the next best thing to the Grace of God for a preacher is oxygen."

Let There Be Light—on Your Face

Unless you are demonstrating Spiritualism before a group of people, flood the room, if possible, with lights. It is as easy to domesticate a quail as to develop enthusiasm in a half-lighted room gloomy as the inside of a thermos bottle.

Read David Belasco's articles on stage production, and you will discover that the average speaker does not have the foggiest shadow of the ghost of an idea of the tremendous importance of proper lighting.

Let the light strike your face. People want to see you.

The subtle changes that ought to play across your features are a part, and a very real part, of the process of self-expression. Sometimes they mean more than your words. If you stand directly under a light, your face may be dimmed by a shadow; if you stand directly in front of a light, it is sure to be. Would it not, then, be the part of wisdom to select, before you arise to speak, the spot that will give you the most advantageous illumination?

No Trumpery on the Platform

And do not hide behind a table. People want to look at the whole man. They will even lean out in the aisles to see all of him.

Some well-meaning soul is pretty sure to give you a table and a water pitcher and a glass; but if your throat becomes dry, a pinch of salt or a taste of lemon will start the saliva again better than Niagara.

You do not want the water nor the pitcher. Neither do you want all the other useless and ugly impedimenta that clutter up the average platform.

The Broadway salesrooms of the various automobile makers are beautiful, orderly, pleasing to the eye. The Paris offices of the large perfumers and jewelers are artistically and luxuriously appointed. Why? It is good business. One has more respect, more confidence, more admiration for a concern housed like that.

For the same reason, a speaker ought to have a pleasing background. The ideal arrangement, to my way of thinking, would be no furniture at all. Nothing behind the speaker to attract attention, or at either side of him—nothing but a curtain of dark blue velvet.

But what does he usually have behind him? Maps and signs and tables, perhaps a lot of dusty chairs, some piled on top of the others. And what is the result? A cheap, slovenly, disorderly atmosphere. So clear all the trumpery away.

"The most important thing in public speaking," said Henry Ward Beecher, "is the man."

So let the speaker stand out like the snowclad tops of the Jungfrau towering against the blue skies of Switzerland.

No Guests on the Platform

I was once in London, Ontario, when the Prime Minister of Canada was speaking. Presently the janitor, armed with a long pole, started to ventilate the room, moving about from window to window. What happened? The audience, almost to a man, ignored the speaker for a little while and stared at the janitor as intently as if he had been performing some miracle.

An audience cannot resist—or, what comes to the same thing, it *will not* resist—the temptation to look at moving objects. If a speaker will only remember that truth, he can save himself some trouble and needless annoyance.

First, he can refrain from twiddling his thumbs, playing with his clothes and making little nervous movements that detract from him. I remember seeing a New York audience watch a well-known speaker's hands for half an hour while he spoke and played with the covering of a pulpit at the same time.

Second, the speaker should arrange, if possible, to have the audience seated so they won't have their attention distracted by seeing the late comers enter.

Third, he should have no guests on the platform. A few years ago Raymond Robins delivered a series of talks in Brooklyn. Along with a number of others, I was invited to sit on the platform with him. I declined on the ground that it was unfair to the speaker. I noted the first night how many of these guests shifted about and put one leg over the other and back again, and so on; and every time one of them moved, the audience looked away from the speaker to the guest. I called Mr. Robins' attention to this the next day; and during the remainder of his evenings with us, he very wisely occupied the platform alone.

David Belasco did not permit the use of red flowers on the stage because they attract too much attention. Then why should a speaker permit a restless human being to sit facing the audience while he talks? He shouldn't. And, if he is wise, he won't.

The Art of Sitting Down

Isn't it well for the speaker himself not to sit facing the audience before he begins? Isn't it better to arrive as a fresh exhibit than an old one?

But, if we *must* sit, let us be careful of *how* we sit. You have seen men look around to find a chair with the modified movements of a foxhound lying down for the night. They turned around and when they did locate a chair, they doubled up and flopped down into it with all the self-control of a sack of sand.

A man who knows how to sit feels the chair strike the back of his legs, and, with his body easily erect from head to hips, he *sinks* into it with his body under perfect control.

Poise

We just said, a few pages previously, not to play with your clothes or your jewelry because it attracted attention. There is another reason also. It gives an impression of weakness, a lack of self-control. Every movement that does not add to your presence detracts from it. There are no neutral movements. None. So stand still and control yourself physically and that will give you an impression of mental control, of poise.

After you have risen to address your audience, do not be in a hurry to begin. That is the hallmark of the amateur. Take a deep breath. Look over your audience for a moment; and, if there is a noise or disturbance, pause until it quiets down.

Hold your chest high. But why wait until you get before an audience to do this? Why not do it daily in private? Then you will do it unconsciously in public.

"Not one man in ten," said Luther H. Gulick in his book, *The Efficient Life,* "carries himself so as to look his best. . . . Keep the neck pressed against the collar." Here is a daily exercise he recommends: "Inhale slowly and as strongly as possible. At the same time press the neck back firmly against the collar. Now hold it there hard. There is no harm in doing this in an exaggerated way. The object is to straighten out that part of the back which is directly between the shoulders. This deepens the chest."

And what shall you do with your hands? Forget them. If they fall naturally to your sides, that is ideal. If they feel like a bunch of bananas to you, do not be deluded into imagining that anyone else is paying the slightest attention to them or has the slightest interest in them.

They will look best hanging relaxed at your sides. They will attract the minimum of attention there. Not even the hypercritical can criticize that position. Besides, they will be unhampered and free to flow naturally into gestures when the urge makes itself felt.

But suppose that you are very nervous and that you find putting them behind your back, shoving them into your pockets or resting them on the rostrum, helps to relieve your self-consciousness—what should you do? Use your common sense. I have heard a number of the celebrated speakers of this generation. Many, if not most, put their hands into their pockets occasionally while speaking. Bryan did it. Chauncey M. Depew did it. Teddy Roosevelt did it. Even so fastidious a dandy as Disraeli sometimes succumbed to this temptation. But the sky did not fall and, according to the weather reports, if my memory serves me right, the sun came up on time as usual the next morning. If a person has something to say worth while, and says it with contagious conviction, surely it will matter little what he does with his hands and feet. If his head is full and heart stirred, these secondary details will very largely take care of themselves. After all, the stupendously important thing in making a talk is the psychological aspect of it, not the position of the hands and feet.

Absurd Antics Taught in the Name of Gesture

And this brings us very naturally to the much-abused question of gesture. My first lesson in public speaking was given by the president of a college in the Middle West. This lesson, as I remember it, was chiefly concerned with gesturing; it was not only useless but misleading and positively harmful. I was taught to let my arm hang loosely at my side, palm facing the rear, fingers half closed and thumb touching my leg. I was drilled to bring the arm up in a graceful curve, to make a classical swing with the wrist and then to unfold the forefinger first, the second finger next, and the little finger last. When the whole aesthetic and ornamental movement had been executed, the arm was then to retrace the same graceful and unnatural curve and rest again by the side of the leg. The whole performance was wooden and affected. There was nothing sensible or honest about it. I was drilled to act as no one, in his right mind, ever acted anywhere.

There was no attempt whatever to get me to put my own individuality into my movements; no attempt to spur me on to feeling like gesturing; no endeavor to get the flow and blood of life in the process, and make it natural and unconscious and inevitable; no urging me to let go, to be spontaneous, to break through my shell of reserve, to talk and act like a human being. No, the whole regrettable performance was as mechanical as a typewriter, as lifeless as a last year's bird nest, as ridiculous as a Punch and Judy show.

It seems incredible that such absurd antics could have been taught in the twentieth century, yet only a few years ago a book about gesturing was published—a whole book trying to make automatons out of men, telling them which gesture to make on this sentence, which to make on that, which to make with one hand, which with both, which to make high, which to make medium, which to make low, how to hold this finger and how to hold that. I have seen twenty men at a time standing before a class, all reading the same ornate oratorical selection from such a book, all making precisely the same gestures on precisely the same words, and all making themselves precisely ridiculous. Artificial, time-killing, mechanical, injurious—it has brought this whole subject into disrepute with many people. The dean of a large college in Massachusetts recently said that his institution had no course in public speaking because he had never seen one that was practical, one that taught how to speak sensibly. My sympathy was all with the dean.

Nine-tenths of the stuff that has been written on gestures has been a waste and worse than a waste of good white paper and good black ink. Any gesture that is gotten out of a book is very likely to look like it. The place to get it is out of yourself, out of your heart, out of your mind, out of your own interest in the subject, out of your own desire to make someone else see as you see, out of your own impulses. The only gestures that are worth one, two, three, are those that are born on the spur of the instant. An ounce of spontaneity is worth a ton of rules.

Gesture is not a thing to be put on at will like a dinner jacket. It is merely an outward expression of inward condition just as are kisses and colic and laughter and seasickness.

And a man's gestures, like his toothbrush, should be very personal things. And, as all people are different, their gestures will be individual if they will only act natural.

No two persons should be drilled to gesture in precisely the same fashion. Imagine trying to make the long, awkward slow-thinking Lincoln gesture in the same fashion as did the rapidly-talking, impetuous and polished Douglas. It would be ridiculous.

"Lincoln," according to his biographer and law partner, Herndon, "did not gesticulate as much with his hands as with his head. He used the latter frequently, throwing it with vim this way and that. This movement was a significant one when he sought to enforce his statement. It sometimes came with a quick jerk, as if throwing off electric sparks into combustible material. He never sawed the air or rent space into tatters and rags as some orators do. He never acted for stage effect. . . . As he moved along in his speech he became freer and less uneasy in his movements; to that extent he was graceful. He had a perfect naturalness, a strong individuality; and to that extent he was dignified. He despised glitter, show, set forms and shams. . . . There was a world of meaning and emphasis in the long, bony finger of his right hand as he dotted the ideas on the minds of his hearers. Sometimes, to express joy or pleasure, he would raise both hands at an angle of about fifty degrees, the palms upward, as if desirous of embracing the spirit of that which he loved. If the sentiment was one of detestation—denunciation of slavery, for example—both arms, thrown upward and fists clenched, swept through the air, and he expressed an execration that was truly sublime. This was one of his most effective gestures, and signified most vividly a fixed determination to drag down the object of his hatred and trample it in the dust. He always stood squarely on his feet, toe even with toe; that is, he never put one foot before the other. He neither touched nor leaned on anything for support. He made but few changes in his positions and attitudes. He never ranted, never walked backward and forward on the platform. To ease his arms, he frequently caught hold, with his left hand, of the lapel of his coat, keeping his thumb upright and leaving his right hand free to gesticulate." St. Gaudens caught him in just that attitude in the statue which stands in Lincoln Park, Chicago.

Such was Lincoln's method. Theodore Roosevelt was more vigorous, fiery, active, his whole face alive with feeling, his fist clenched, his entire body an instrument of expression. Bryan often used the outstretched hand with open palm. Gladstone often struck a table or his open palm with his fist, or stamped his foot with a resounding thud on the floor. Lord Rosebery used to raise his right arm and bring it down with a bold sweep that had tremendous force. Ah, but there was force first in the speaker's thoughts and convictions; that was what made the gesture strong and spontaneous.

Spontaneity . . . life . . . they are the *summum bonum* of action. Burke was angular and exceedingly awkward in his gestures. Pitt sawed the air with his arms "like a clumsy clown." Sir Henry Irving was handicapped by a lame leg and decidedly odd movements. Lord Macaulay's actions on the platform were ungainly. So were Grattan's. So were Parnell's. "The answer then appears to be," said the late Lord Curzon at Cambridge University, in an address on Parliamentary Eloquence, "that great public speakers make their own gestures; and that while a great orator is doubtless aided by a handsome exterior and graceful action, it does not matter very much if he happens to be ugly and awkward."

Many years ago, I heard the famous Gypsy Smith preach. I was enthralled by the eloquence of this man who had led so many thousands to Christ. He used gestures—lots of them—and was no more conscious of them than of the air he breathed. Such is the ideal way.

And such is the way you will find yourself making gestures if you will but practice and apply these principles. I can't give you any rules for gesturing, for everything depends upon the temperament of the speaker, upon his preparation, his enthusiasm, his personality, the subject, the audience, the occasion.

Suggestions That May Prove Helpful

Here are, however, a few limited suggestions that may prove useful. Do not repeat one gesture until it becomes monotonous. Do not make short, jerky movements from the elbow. The movements from the shoulder look better on the platform. Do not end your gestures too quickly. If you are using the index finger to drive home your thought, do not be afraid to hold that gesture through an entire sentence. The failure to do this is a very common error and a serious one. It distorts your emphasis, making small things unimportant, and truly important points seem trivial by comparison.

When you are doing real speaking before a real audience, make only the gestures that come natural. But while you are practicing, *force* yourself, if necessary, to use gestures. Force yourself to do it, and the doing of it will so awaken and stimulate you that your gestures will soon be coming unsought.

Shut your book. You can't learn gestures from a printed page. Your own impulses, as you are speaking, are more to be trusted, more valuable than anything any instructor can possibly tell you.

If you forget all else we have said about gesture and delivery, remember this: if a man is so wrapped up in what he has to say, if he is so eager to get his message across that he forgets himself and talks and acts spontaneously, then his gestures and his delivery, unstudied though they may be, are very likely to be almost above criticism. If you doubt this, walk up to a man and knock him down. You will probably discover that, when he regains his feet, the talk he delivers will be well nigh flawless as a gem of eloquence.

Here are the best eleven words I have ever read on the subject of delivery:

> Fill up the barrel.
> Knock out the bung.
> Let nature caper.

Summary

1. According to experiments conducted by the Carnegie Institute of Technology, personality has more to do with business success than has superior knowledge. This pronouncement is as true of speaking as of business. Personality, however, is such an intangible, elusive, mysterious thing that it is almost impossible to give directions for developing it, but some of the suggestions given in this chapter will help a speaker to appear at his best.

2. Don't speak when you are tired. Rest, recuperate, store up a reserve of energy.

3. Eat sparingly before you speak.

4. Do nothing to dull your energy. It is magnetic. People cluster around the energetic speaker like wild geese around a field of autumn wheat.

5. Dress neatly, attractively. The consciousness of being well dressed heightens one's self-respect, increases self-confidence. If a speaker has baggy trousers, unkempt shoes, ungroomed hair, fountain pen and pencils peeping out of his coat pocket, or a bulging, ugly handbag, the audience is liable to feel as little respect for the person as he seems to feel for himself.

6. Smile. Come before your hearers with an attitude that seems to say you are glad to be there. "Like begets like," says Professor Overstreet. "If we are interested in our audience there is every likelihood that our audience will be interested in us. Even before we speak, very often, we are condemned or approved. There is every reason, therefore, that we should make certain that our attitude is such as to elicit warm response."

7. Crowd your audience together. No group is easily in-

fluenced when it is scattered. An individual, as a member of a compact audience, will laugh at, applaud and approve things that he might question and oppose if he were addressed singly or if he were one of a group scattered through a large room.

8. If you are speaking to a small group, pack them in a small room. Don't stand on a platform. Get down on the same level with them. Make your talk intimate, informal, conversational.

9. Keep the air fresh.

10. Flood the place with lights. Stand so that the light will fall directly in your face, so all your features can be seen.

11. Don't stand behind furniture. Push the tables and chairs to one side. Clear away all the unsightly signs and trumpery that often clutter up a platform.

12. If you have guests on the platform, they are sure to move occasionally; and, each time they make the slightest movement, they are certain to seize the attention of your hearers. An audience cannot resist the temptation to look at any moving object or animal or person; so why store up trouble and create competition for yourself?

CHAPTER EIGHT

How to Open a Talk

I once asked Dr. Lynn Harold Hough, formerly president of Northwestern University, what was the most important fact that his long experience as a speaker had taught him. After pondering for a minute, he replied, "To get an arresting opening, something that will seize the attention immediately." He planned in advance almost the precise words of both his opening and closing. John Bright did the same thing. Gladstone did it. Webster did it. Lincoln did it. Practically every speaker with common sense and experience does it.

But does the beginner? Seldom. Planning takes time, requires thought, demands will power. Cerebration is a painful process. Thomas Edison had this quotation from Sir Joshua Reynolds nailed on the walls of his plants:

> There is no expedient to which a man will not resort to avoid the real labor of thinking.

The tyro usually trusts to the inspiration of the moment with the consequence that he finds:

> Beset with pitfall and with gin,
> The road he is to wander in.

The late Lord Northcliffe, who fought his way up from a meager weekly salary to being the richest and most influential newspaper owner in the British Empire, said that these five words from Pascal had done more to help him succeed than anything else he had ever read:

To foresee is to rule.

That is also a most excellent motto to have on your desk when you are planning your talk. Foresee how you are going to begin when the mind is fresh to grasp every word you utter. Foresee what impression you are going to leave last—when nothing else follows to obliterate it.

Ever since the days of Aristotle, books on this subject have divided the speech into three sections: the introduction, the body, the conclusion. Until comparatively recently, the introduction often was, and could really afford to be, as leisurely as a buggy ride. The speaker then was both a bringer of news and an entertainer. A hundred years ago he often filled the niche in the community that is filled today by the newspaper, the magazine, the radio, television, the telephone, the movie theater.

But conditions have altered amazingly. The world has been made over. Inventions have speeded up life more in the last hundred years than they had formerly in all the ages since Belshazzar and Nebuchadnezzar. Automobiles, aeroplanes, radio, television; we are moving with increasing speed. And the speaker must fall in line with the impatient tempo of the times. If you are going to use an introduction, believe me, it ought to be short as a billboard advertisement. This is about the temper of the average modern audience: "Got anything to say? All right, let's have it quickly and with very little trimmings. No oratory! Give us the facts quickly and sit down."

When Woodrow Wilson addressed Congress on such a momentous question as an ultimatum on submarine warfare, he announced his topic and centered the audience's attention on the subject with just twenty-three words:

A situation has arisen in the foreign relations of

the country of which it is my plain duty to inform you very frankly.

When Charles Schwab addressed the Pennsylvania Society of New York, he strode right into the heart of his talk with his second sentence:

> Uppermost in the minds of American citizens to-day is the question: What is the meaning of the existing slump in business and what of the future? Personally, I am an optimist. . . .

The salesmanager for the National Cash Register Company opened one of his talks to his men in this fashion. Only three sentences in this introduction; and they are all easy to listen to, they all have vigor and drive:

> You men who get the orders are the chaps who are supposed to keep the smoke coming out of the factory chimney. The volume of smoke emitted from our chimney during the past two summer months hasn't been large enough to darken the landscape to any great extent. Now that the dog days are over and the business-revival season has begun, we are addressing to you a short, sharp request on this subject: We want more smoke.

But do inexperienced speakers usually achieve such commendable swiftness and succinctness in their openings? The majority of untrained and unskilled speakers will begin in one of two ways—both of which are bad. Let us discuss them forthwith.

Beware of Opening with a So-called Humorous Story

For some lamentable reason, the novice often feels that he ought to be funny as a speaker. He may, by nature, mind you, be as solemn as the encyclopedia, utterly devoid of the lighter touch; yet the moment he stands up to talk he imagines he feels, or ought to feel, the spirit of Mark Twain descending upon him. So he is inclined to open with a humorous story, especially if the occcasion is an after-dinner affair. What happens? The chances are twenty to one that the narration, the manner of this newly turned raconteur, is as heavy as the dictionary. The chances are his stories don't "click." In the immortal language of the immortal Hamlet, they prove "weary, stale, flat and unprofitable."

If an entertainer were to misfire a few times like that before an audience that had paid for their seats, they would "boo" and shout "give him the hook." But the average group listening to a speaker is very sympathetic; so, out of sheer charity, they will do their best to manufacture a few chuckles; while, deep in their hearts, they pity the would-be humorous speaker for his failure! They themselves feel uncomfortable. Haven't you witnessed this kind of fiasco time after time?

In all the difficult realm of speech making, what is more difficult, more rare, than the ability to make an audience laugh? Humor is a hair trigger affair; it is so much a matter of individuality, of personality.

Remember, it is seldom the story that is funny of, by, and in itself. It is the way it is told that makes it a success. Ninety-nine men out of a hundred will fail woefully with the identical stories that made Mark Twain famous. Read the stories that Lincoln repeated in the taverns of the Eighth Judicial District of Illinois, stories that men drove miles to hear, stories that men sat up all night to hear, stories that, according to an eye witness, sometimes caused the natives to "whoop and roll off their chairs." Read those stories aloud to your family and see if you conjure up a smile. Here is one Lincoln used to tell with roaring success. Why not try it? Privately, please—not before an audience. A late traveler, trying to reach home over the muddy roads of the Illinois prairies, was overtaken by a storm. The night was black as ink; the rain descended as if some dam in the heavens had broken; thunder rent the angry clouds like the explosion of dynamite. Chain lightning showed trees falling around. The roar of it was very nearly deafening. Finally, a crash more terrific, more terrible, than any the helpless man had ever heard in his life, brought him to his knees. He was not given to praying, usually, but "Oh, Lord," he gasped, "if it is all the same to you, please give us a little more light and a little less noise."

You may be one of those fortunately endowed individuals who has the rare gift of humor. If so, by all means, cultivate it. You will be thrice welcome wherever you speak. But if your talent lies in other directions, it is folly—and it ought to be high treason—for you to attempt to wear the mantle of Chauncey M. Depew.

Were you to study his speeches, and Lincoln's, and Job Hedges', you would probably be surprised at the few stories they told, especially in their openings. Edwin James Cattell confided to me that he had never told a funny story for the mere sake of humor. It had to be relevant, had to illustrate a point. Humor ought to be merely the frosting on the cake, merely the chocolate between the layers, not the cake itself. Strickland Gillilan, one of the best humorous lecturers in these United States, made it a rule never to tell a story during the first three minutes of his talk. If he found that practice advisable, I wonder if you and I would not also.

Must the opening, then, be heavy-footed, elephantine and excessively solemn? Not at all. Tickle our risibilities, if you can, by some local reference, something anent the occasion or the remarks of some other speaker. Observe some incongruity. Exaggerate it. That brand of humor is forty times more likely to succeed than stale jokes about Pat and Mike, or a mother-in-law, or a goat.

Perhaps the easiest way to create merriment is to tell a joke on yourself. Depict yourself in some ridiculous and embarrassing situation. That gets down to the very essence of much humor. The Eskimos laugh even at a chap who has broken his leg. The Chinese chuckle over the dog that has fallen out of a second story window and killed himself. We are a bit more sympathetic than that, but don't we smile at the fellow chasing his hat, or slipping on a banana skin?

Almost anyone can make an audience laugh by grouping incongruous ideas or qualities as, for example, the statement of a newspaper writer that he "hated children, tripe, and Democrats."

Note how cleverly Rudyard Kipling raised laughs in this opening to one of his political talks in England. He is retailing here, not manufactured anecdotes, but some of his own experiences and playfully stressing their incongruities:

> My Lords, Ladies and Gentlemen: When I was a young man in India I used to report criminal cases for the newspaper that employed me. It was interesting work because it introduced me to forgers and embezzlers and murderers and enterprising sportsmen of that kind. (Laughter.) Sometimes, after I had reported their trials, I used to visit my friends in jail when they were doing their sentences. (Laughter.) I remember one man who got off with a life sentence for murder. He was a clever, smooth-speaking chap, and he told me what he called the story of his life. He said: "Take it from me that when a man gets crooked, one thing leads to another until he finds himself in such a position that he has to put somebody out of the way to get straight again." (Laughter.) Well, that exactly describes the present position of the cabinet. (Laughter and cheers.)

This is the way William Howard Taft managed a bit of humor at the annual banquet of the superintendents of the Metropolitan Life Insurance Company. The beautiful part of it is this: he is humorous and pays his audience a gracious compliment at the same time:

> *Mr. President and Gentlemen of the Metropolitan Life Insurance Company:*
>
> I was out in my old home about nine months ago, and I heard an after-dinner speech there by a gentleman who had some trepidation in making it; and he said he had consulted a friend of his, who had had a great deal of experience in making after-dinner speeches, which friend advised him that the best kind of audience to address, as an after-dinner speaker, was an audience in-

telligent and well-educated but half-tight. (Laughter and applause.) Now, all I can say is that this audience is one of the best audiences I ever saw for an after-dinner speaker. Something has made up for the absence of that element that the remark implied (applause), and I must think it is the spirit of the Metropolitan Life Insurance Company. (Prolonged applause.)

Do Not Begin with an Apology

The second egregious blunder that the beginner is wont to make in his opening, is this: He apologizes. "I am no speaker. . . . I am not prepared to talk. . . . I have nothing to say. . . ."

Don't! Don't! The opening words of a poem by Kipling are: "There's no use in going further." That is precisely the way an audience feels when a speaker opens in that fashion.

Anway, if you are not prepared, some of us will discover it without your assistance. Others will not. Why call their attention to it? Why insult your audience by suggesting that you did not think them worth preparing for, that just any old thing you happened to have on the fire would be good enough to serve them? No. No. We don't want to hear your apologies. We are there to be informed and interested, to be *interested,* remember that.

The moment you come before the audience, you have our attention naturally, inevitably. It is not difficult to get it for the next five seconds, but it is difficult to hold it for the next five minutes. If you once lose it, it will be doubly difficult to win it back. So begin with something interesting in your very first sentence. Not the second. Not the third. The first! F-I-R-S-T. First!

"How?" you ask. Rather a large order, I admit. And in attempting to harvest the material to fill it, we must tread our way down devious and dubious paths, for so much depends upon you, upon your audience, your subject, your material, the occasion, and so on. However, we hope that the tentative suggestions discussed and illustrated in the remainder of this chapter will yield something usable and of value.

Arouse Curiosity

Here is an opening used by Mr. Howell Healy in a talk given at the Penn Athletic Club, Philadelphia. Do you like it? Does it get your interest immediately?

> Eighty-two years ago, and just about this time of year, there was published in London a little volume, a story, which was destined to become immortal. Many people have called it "the greatest little book in the world." When it first appeared, friends meeting one another on the Strand or Pall Mall, asked the question, "Have you read it?" The answer invariably was: "Yes, God bless him, I have."
>
> The day it was published a thousand copies were sold. Within a fortnight, the demand had consumed fifteen thousand. Since then it has run into countless editions, and has been translated into every language under heaven. A few years ago J. P. Morgan purchased the original manuscript for a fabulous sum; it now reposes among his other priceless treasures in that magnificent art gallery in New York City which he calls his library.
>
> What is this world-famous book? Dickens' *Christmas Carol*. . . .

Do you consider that a successful opening? Did it hold your attention, heighten your interest as it progressed? Why? Was it not because it aroused your curiosity, held you in suspense?

Curiosity! Who is not susceptible to it?

I have seen birds in the woods fly about by the hour watching me out of sheer curiosity. I know a hunter in the high Alps who lures chamois by throwing a bed sheet around him and crawling about and arousing their curiosity. Dogs have curiosity, and so have kittens, and all manner of animals including the well-known *genus homo.*

So arouse your audience's curiosity with your first sentence, and you have their interested attention.

The writer used to begin his lecture on Colonel Thomas Lawrence's adventures in Arabia in this fashion:

> Lloyd George says that he regards Colonel Lawrence as one of the most romantic and picturesque characters of modern times.

That opening had two advantages. In the first place, a quotation from an eminent man always has a lot of attention value. Second, it aroused curiosity: "Why romantic?" was the natural question, and "why picturesque?" "I never heard about him before. . . . What did he do?"

Lowell Thomas began his lecture on Colonel Thomas Lawrence with this statement:

> I was going down Christian Street in Jerusalem one day when I met a man clad in the gorgeous robes of an oriental potentate; and, at his side, hung the curved gold sword worn only by the descendants of the prophet Mohammed. But this man had none of the appearances of an Arab. He had blue eyes; and the Arabs' eyes are always black or brown.

That piques your curiosity, doesn't it? You want to hear more. Who was he? Why was he posing as an Arab? What did he do? What became of him?

The student who opened his talk with this question:

> Do you know that slavery exists in seventeen nations of the world today?

not only aroused curiosity, but in addition, he shocked his auditors. "Slavery? Today? Seventeen countries? Seems incredible. What nations? Where are they?"

One can often arouse curiosity by beginning with an effect, and making people anxious to hear the cause. For example, one student began with this striking statement:

> A member of one of our legislatures recently stood up in his legislative assembly and proposed the passage of a law prohibiting tadpoles from becoming frogs within two miles of any schoolhouse.

You smile. Is the speaker joking? How absurd. Was that actually done? . . . Yes. The speaker went on to explain.

An article in *The Saturday Evening Post,* entitled "With The Gangsters," began:

> Are gangsters really organized? As a rule they are. How? . . .

With ten words, you see, the writer of that article announced his subject, told you something about it, and aroused your curiosity as to how gangsters are organized. Very creditable. Every person who aspires to speak in public ought to study the technique that magazine writers employ to hook the reader's interest immediately. You can learn far more from them about how to open a speech than you can by studying collections of printed speeches.

Why Not Begin with a Story?

We especially like to hear a speaker relate narratives from his own experience. Russell E. Conwell delivered his lecture, "Acres of Diamonds," over six thousand times, and received millions for it. And how does this marvelously popular lecture begin?

> In 1870 we went down the Tigris River. We hired a guide at Bagdad to show us Persepolis, Nineveh, and Babylon. . . .

And he is off—with a *story.* That is what hooks the attention. That kind of opening is almost foolproof. It can hardly fail. It moves. It marches. We follow. We want to know what is going to happen.

The story-opening was used to launch Chapter III of this book.

Here are opening sentences taken from two stories that appeared in a single issue of *The Saturday Evening Post:*

> 1. The sharp crack of a revolver punctuated the silence.
>
> 2. An incident, trivial in itself but not at all trivial in its possible consequences, occurred at the Montview Hotel, Denver, during the first week of July. It so aroused the curiosity of Goebel, the resident manager, that he referred it to Steve Faraday, owner of the Montview and half a dozen other Faraday hotels, when Steve made his regular visit a few days later on his midsummer swing of inspection.

Note that those openings have action. They start something. They arouse your curiosity. You want to read on; you want to know more; you want to find out what it is all about.

Even the unpracticed beginner can usually manage a succeessful opening if he employs the story technique and arouses our curiosity.

Begin with a Specific Illustration

It is difficult, it is arduous, for the average audience to follow abstract statements very long. Illustrations are easier to listen to, far easier. Then, why not start with one? It is hard to get speakers to do that. I know. I have tried. They feel somehow that they must first make a few general statements. Not at all. Open with your illustration, arouse the interest; then follow with your general remarks. If you wish an example of this technique, please turn to the opening of Chapter VI.

What technique was employed to open this chapter you are now reading?

Use an Exhibit

Perhaps the easiest way in the world to gain attention is to hold up something for people to look at. Even savages and half-wits, and babes in the cradle and monkeys in a store window and dogs on the street will give heed to that kind of stimulus. It can be used sometimes with effectiveness before the most dignified audience. For example, Mr. S. S. Ellis, of Philadelphia, opened one of his talks by holding a coin between his thumb and forefinger, and high above his shoulder. Naturally everyone looked. Then he inquired: "Has anyone here ever found a coin like this on the sidewalk? It announces that the fortunate finder will be given a lot free in such and such a real estate development. He has but to call and present this coin. . . ." Mr. Ellis then proceeded to condemn the misleading and unethical practices involved.

Ask a Question

Mr. Ellis' opening has another commendable feature. It begins by asking a question, by getting the audience thinking with the speaker, coöperating with him. Note that *The Saturday Evening Post* article on gangsters opens with two questions in the first three sentences: "Are gangsters really organized? . . . How?" The use of this question-key is really one of the simplest, surest ways to unlock the minds of your audience and let yourself in. When other tools prove useless, you can always fall back on it.

Why Not Open with a Question from Some Famous Man?

The words of a prominent man always have attention power; so a suitable quotation is one of the very best ways of launching a harangue. Do you like the following opening of a discussion on Business Success?

> "The world bestows its big prizes both in money and honors for but one thing," says Elbert Hubbard. "And that is initiative. And what is initiative? I'll tell you: it is doing the right thing without being told."

As a starter, that has several commendable features. The initial sentence arouses curiosity; it carries us forward, we want to hear more. If the speaker pauses skillfully after the words, "Elbert Hubbard," it arouses suspense. "What does the world bestow its big prizes for?" we ask. Quick. Tell us. We may not agree with you, but give us your opinion anyway. . . . The second sentence leads us right into the heart of the subject. The third sentence, a question, invites the audience to get in on the discussion, to think, to do a little something. And how audiences like to do things. They love it! The fourth sentence defines initiative. . . . After this opening the speaker led off with a human interest story illustrating that quality. As far as construction is concerned, Moody might have rated the stock of that talk A*aa.*

Tie Your Topic Up to the Vital Interests of Your Hearers

Begin on some note that goes straight to the personal interests of the audience. That is one of the best of all possible ways to start. It is sure to get attention. We are mightily interested in the things that touch us significantly, momentously.

That is only common sense, isn't it? Yet the use of it is very uncommon. For example, I heard a speaker begin a talk on the necessity of periodic health examinations. How did he open? By telling the history of the Life Extension Institute, how it was organized and the service it was rendering. Absurd! Our hearers have not the foggiest, not the remotest, interest in how some company somewhere was formed; but they are stupendously and eternally interested in themselves.

Why not recognize that fundamental fact? Why not show how that company is of vital concern to them? Why not begin something like this? "Do you know how long you are expected to live according to life insurance tables? Your expectancy of life, as insurance statisticians phrase it, is two-thirds of the time between your present age and eighty. For example, if you are thirty-five now, the difference between your present age and eighty is forty-five; you can expect to live two-third of that amount, or another thirty years. . . . Is that enough? No, no, we are all passionately eager for more. Yet those tables are based upon millions of records. May you and I, then, hope to beat them? Yes, with proper precaution, we may; but the very first step is to have a thorough physical examination . . ."

Then, if we explain in detail why the periodic health examination is necessary, the hearer might be interested in some company formed to render that service. But to begin talking about the company in an impersonal way. It is disastrous! Deadly!

Take another example: I heard a student begin a talk on the prime urgency of conserving our forests. He opened like this: "We, as Americans, ought to be proud of our national resources. . . ." From that sentence, he went on to show that we were wasting our timber at a shameless and indefensible pace. But the opening was bad, too general, too vague. He did not make his subject seem vital to us. There was a printer in that audience. The destruction of our forests will mean something very real to his business. There was a banker; it is going to affect him for it will affect our general prosperity . . . and so on. Why not begin, then, by saying: "The subject I am going to speak about affects your business, Mr. Appleby; and yours, Mr. Saul. In fact, it will, in some measure, affect the price of the food we eat and the rent that we pay. It touches the welfare and prosperity of us all."

Is that exaggerating the importance of conserving our forests? No, I think not. It is only obeying Elbert Hubbard's injunction to "paint the picture large and put the matter in a way that compels attention."

The Attention Power of Shocking Facts

"A good magazine article," said S. S. McClure, the founder of an important periodical, "is a series of shocks."

They jar us out of our daydreams; they seize, they demand attention. Here are some illustrations: Mr. N. D. Ballantine, of Baltimore, began his address on *The Marvels of Radio* with this statement:

> Do you realize that the sound of a fly walking across a pane of glass in New York can be broadcast by radio and made to roar away off in Central Africa like the falls of Niagara?

Mr. Harry G. Jones, president of Harry G. Jones Company, of New York City, began his talk on the *Criminal Situation* with these words:

> "The administration of our criminal law," declared William Howard Taft, then Chief Justice of the Supreme Court of the United States, "is a disgrace to civilization."

That has the double advantage of being not only a shocking opening, but the shocking statement is quoted from an authority on jurisprudence.

Mr. Paul Gibbons, former president of the Optimist Club of Philadelphia, opened an address on *Crime* with these arresting statements:

> The American people are the worst criminals in the world. Astounding as that assertion is, it is true. Cleveland, Ohio, has six times as many murders as all London. It has one hundred and seventy times as many robberies, according to its population, as has London. More people are robbed every year, or assaulted with intent

> to rob, in Cleveland than in all England, Scotland and Wales combined. More people are murdered every year in St. Louis than in all England and Wales. There are more murders in New York City than in all France or German or Italy or the British Isles. The sad truth of the matter is that the criminal is not punished. If you commit a murder, there is less than one chance in a hundred that you will ever be executed for it. You, as a peaceful citizen, are ten times as liable to die from cancer as you would be to be hanged if you shot a man.

That opening was successful, for Mr. Gibbons put the requisite power and earnestness behind his words. They lived. They breathed. However, I have heard other students begin their talks on the crime situation with somewhat similar illustrations; yet their openings were mediocre. Why? Words. Words. Words. Their technique of construction was flawless, but their spirit was nil. Their manner vitiated and emaciated all they said.

The Value of the Seemingly Casual Opening

How do you like the following opening, and why? Mary E. Richmond is addressing the annual meeting of the New York League of Women Voters in the days before legislation against child marriages:

> Yesterday, as the train passed through a city not far from here, I was reminded of a marriage that took place there a few years ago. Because many other marriages in this state have been just as hasty and disastrous as this one, I am going to begin what I have to say to-day with some of the details of this individual instance.
>
> It was on December 12th that a high school girl of fifteen in that city met for the first time a junior in a nearby college who had just attained his majority. On December 15th, only three days later, they procured a marriage license by swearing that the girl was eighteen and was therefore free from the necessity of procuring

> parental consent. Leaving the city clerk's office with their license, they applied at once to a priest (the girl was a Catholic), but very properly he refused to marry them. In some way, perhaps through this priest, the child's mother received news of the attempted marriage. Before she could find her daughter, however, a justice of the peace had united the pair. The bridegroom then took his bride to a hotel where they spent two days and two nights, at the end of which time he abandoned her and never lived with her again.

Personally, I like that opening very much. The very first sentence is good. It forecasts an interesting reminiscence. We want to hear the details. We settle down to listen to a human interest story. In addition to that, it seems very natural. It does not smack of the study, it is not formal, it does not smell of the lamp. . . . "Yesterday, as the train passed through a city not far from here, I was reminded of a marriage that took place there a few years ago." Sounds natural, spontaneous, human. Sounds like one person relating an interesting story to another. An audience likes that. But it is very liable to shy at something too elaborate, something that reeks of preparation with malice aforethought. We want the art that conceals art.

Summary

1. The opening of a talk is difficult. It is also highly important, for the minds of our hearers are fresh then and comparatively easy to impress. It is of too much consequence to be left to chance; it ought to be carefully worked out in advance.

2. The introduction ought to be short, only a sentence or two. Often it can be dispensed with altogether. Wade right into the heart of your subject with the smallest possible number of words. No one objects to that.

3. Novices are prone to begin either with attempting to tell a humorous story or by making an apology. Both of these are usually bad. Very few people—very, very, very few—can relate a humorous anecdote successfully. The attempt usually embarrasses the audience instead of entertaining them. Stories should be relevant, not dragged in just for the sake of the story. Humor should be the icing on the cake, not the cake itself. . . . Never apologize. It is usually an insult to your audience; it bores them. Drive right into what you have to say, say it quickly and sit down.

4. A speaker may be able to win the immediate attention of his audience by:

a. Arousing curiosity. (Illustration: Story of Dickens' *Christmas Carol.*)

b. Relating a human interest story. (Illustration: "Acres of Diamonds" lecture.)

c. Beginning with a specific illustration. (See the opening of Chapter VI of this book.)

d. Using an exhibit. (Illustration: The coin that entitled the finder to a free lot.)

e. Asking a question. (Illustration: "Has any one here ever found a coin like this on the sidewalk?")

f. Opening with a striking quotation. (Illustration: Elbert Hubbard on the Value of Initiative.)

g. Showing how the topic affects the vital interest of the audience. (Illustration: "Your expectancy of life is two-thirds of the amount of time between your present age and eighty. You may be able to increase that by having periodic health examinations," etc.)

h. Starting with shocking facts. (Illustration: "The American people are the worst criminals in the civilized world.")

5. Don't make your opening too formal. Don't let the bones show. Make it appear free, casual, inevitable. This can be done by referring to something that has just happened, or something that has just been said. (Illustration: "Yesterday, as the train passed through a city not far from here, I was reminded . . .")

CHAPTER NINE

How to Close a Talk

Would you like to know in what parts of your speech you are most likely to reveal inexperience or expertness, inaptitude or finesse? In the opening and the closing. There is an old saying in the theater, referring, of course, to actors, that goes like this: "By their entrances and their exits shall ye know them."

The beginning and the ending! They are the hardest things in almost any activity to manage adroitly. For example, at a social function aren't the most trying feats the graceful entrance and the graceful leave-taking? In a business interview, aren't the most difficult tasks the winning approach and the successful close?

The close is really the most strategic point in a speech; what one says last, the final words left ringing in the ears when one ceases—these are likely to be remembered longest. Beginners, however, seldom appreciate the importance of this coign of vantage. Their endings often leave much to be desired.

What are their most common errors? Let us discuss a few and search for remedies.

First, there is the man who finishes with "That is about all I have to say on the matter; so I guess I will stop."

That is not an ending. That is a mistake. It reeks of the amateur. It is almost unpardonable. If that is all you have to say, why not round off your talk, and promptly take your seat and stop without talking about stopping. Do that, and the inference that that is all you have to say may, with safety and good taste, be left to the discernment of the audience.

Then there is the speaker who says all he has to say, but he does not know how to stop. I believe it was Josh Billings who advised people to take the bull by the tail instead of the horns, since it would be easier to let go. This speaker has the bull by the frontal extremities, and wants to part company with him, but try as hard as he will, he can't get near a friendly fence or tree. So he finally thrashes about in a circle, covering the same ground repeating himself, leaving a bad impression. . . .

The remedy? An ending has to be planned sometime, doesn't it? Is it the part of wisdom to try to do it after you are facing an audience, while you are under the strain and stress of talking, while your mind must be intent on what you are saying? Or does common sense suggest the advisability of doing it quietly, calmly, beforehand?

Even such accomplished speakers as Webster, Bright, Gladstone, with their admirable command of the English language, felt it necessary to write down and all but memorize the exact words of their closings.

The beginner, if he follows in their footsteps, will seldom have cause to regret it. He ought to know very definitely with what ideas he is going to close. He ought to rehearse the ending several times, using not necessarily the same phraseology during each repitition, but putting the thoughts definitely into words.

An extemporaneous talk, during the process of delivery, sometimes has to be altered very materially, has to be cut and slashed to meet unforseen developments, to harmonize with the reactions of one's hearers; so it is really wise to have two or three closings planned. If one does not fit, another may.

Some speakers never get to the end at all. Along in the middle of their journey, they begin to sputter and misfire like an engine when the gasoline supply is about exhausted; after a few desperate lunges, they come to a complete standstill, a breakdown. They need, of course, better preparation, more practice—more gasoline in the tank.

Many novices stop too abruptly. Their method of closing lacks smoothness, lacks finish. Properly speaking, they have no close; they merely cease suddenly, jerkily. The effect is unpleasant, amateurish. It is as if a friend in a social conversation were to break off brusquely and dart out of the room without a graceful leave-taking.

No less a speaker than Lincoln made that mistake in the original draft of his First Inaugural. That speech was delivered at a tense time. The black storm clouds of dissension and hatred were already milling overhead. A few weeks later, the cyclone of blood and destruction burst upon the nation. Lincoln, addressing his closing words to the people of the South, had intended to end in this fashion:

> In your hands, my dissatisfied fellow-countrymen, and not in mine, is the momentous issue of the civil war. The government will not assail you. You can have no conflict without being yourselves the aggressors. You have no oath registered in heaven to destroy the government, while I have a most solemn one to preserve, protect and defend it. You can forbear the assault upon it. I cannot shrink from the defense of it. With you and not with me is the solemn question of "Shall it be peace or a sword?"

He submitted his speech to Secretary Seward. Seward quite appropriately pointed out that the ending was too blunt, too abrupt, too provocative. So Seward himself tried his hand at a closing; in fact, he wrote two. Lincoln accepted one of them and used it, with slight modifications, in place of the last three sentences of the close he had originally prepared. The result was that his First Inaugural Address now lost its provocative abruptness and rose to a climax of friendliness, of sheer beauty and poetical eloquence:

> I am loth to close. We are not enemies but friends. We must not be enemies. Though passion may have strained, it must not break our bonds of affection. The mystic chords of memory, stretching from every battlefield and patriot's grave to every living heart and hearthstone all over this broad land, will swell the chorus of the Union when again touched, as surely they will be, by the better angel of our nature.

How can a beginner develop the proper *feeling* for the close of an address? By mechanical rules?

No. Like culture, it is too delicate for that. It must be a matter of sensing, almost of intuition. Unless a speaker can *feel* when it is done harmoniously, adroitly, how can he himself hope to do it?

However, this *feeling* can be cultivated; this experience can be developed somewhat, by studying the ways in which accomplished speakers have achieved it. Here is an illustration, the close of an address by the then Prince of Wales before the Empire Club of Toronto:

> I am afraid, gentlemen, that I have departed from my reserve, and talked about myself a good deal too much. But I wanted to tell you, as the largest audience that I have been privileged to address in Canada, what I feel about my position and the responsibility which it entails. I can only assure you that I shall always endeavor to live up to that great responsibility and to be worthy of your trust.

A blind man listening to that talk would *feel* that it was ended. It isn't left dangling in the air like a loose rope. It isn't left ragged and jagged. It is rounded off, it is finished.

The famous Dr. Harry Emerson Fosdick spoke in the Geneva Cathedral of St. Pierre the Sunday after the opening of the sixth assembly of the League of Nations. He chose for his text: "All they that take the sword shall perish with the sword." Note the beautiful and lofty and powerful way in which he brought his sermon to a close:

We cannot reconcile Jesus Christ and war—that is the essence of the matter. That is the challenge which to-day should stir the conscience of Christendom. War is the most colossal and ruinous social sin that afflicts mankind; it is utterly and irremediably unchristian; in its total method and effect it means everything that Jesus did not mean and it means nothing that he did mean; it is a more blatant denial of every Christian doctrine about God and man than all the theoretical atheists on earth ever could devise. It would be worth while, would it not, to see the Christian Church claim as her own this greatest moral issue of our time, to see her lift once more as in our fathers' days, a clear standard against the paganism of this present world and, refusing to hold her conscience at the beck and call of belligerent states, put the kingdom of God above nationalism and call the world to peace? That would not be the denial of patriotism but its apotheosis.

Here to-day, as an American, under this high and hospitable roof, I cannot speak for my government, but both as an American and as a Christian I do speak for millions of my fellow citizens in wishing your great work, in which we believe, for which we pray, our absence from which we painfully regret, the eminent success which it deserves. We work in many ways for the same end—a world organized for peace. Never was an end better worth working for. The alternative is the most appalling catastrophe mankind has ever faced. Like gravitation in the physical realm, the law of the Lord in the moral realm bends for no man and no nation: "All they that take the sword shall perish with the sword."

But this collection of speech endings would not be complete without the majestic tones, the organ-like melody of the close of Lincoln's Second Inaugural. The late Earl Curzon, of Keddleston, Chancellor of Oxford University, declared that this selection was "among the glories and treasures of mankind . . . the purest gold of human eloquence, nay, of eloquence almost divine":

> Fondly do we hope, fervently do we pray, that this mighty scourge of war may speedily pass away. Yet if God wills that it continue until all the wealth piled by the bondsman's two hundred and fifty years of unrequited toil shall be sunk, and until every drop of blood drawn with the lash shall be paid by another drawn with the sword, as was said three thousand years ago, so still it must be said that "the judgments of the Lord are true and righteous altogether."
>
> With malice toward none; with charity for all; with firmness in the right, as God gives us to see the right, let us strive on to finish the work we are in; to bind up the nation's wounds; to care for him who shall have borne the battle, and for his widow and his orphan—to do all which may achieve and cherish a just and lasting peace among ourselves, and with all nations.

You have just read what is, in my opinion, the most beautiful speech ending ever delivered by the lips of mortal man. . . . Do you agree with my estimate? Where, in all the range of speech literature, will you find more humanity, more sheer loveliness, more sympathy?

"Noble as was the Gettysburg Address," says William E. Barton in *Life of Abraham Lincoln,* "this rises to a still higher level of nobility. . . . It is the greatest of the addresses of Abraham Lincoln and registers his intellectual and spiritual power at their highest altitude."

"This was like a sacred poem," wrote Carl Schurz. "No American President had ever spoken words like these to the American people. America had never had a president who had found such words in the depths of his heart."

But you are not going to deliver immortal pronouncements as President in Washington or as Prime Minister in Ottawa or Canberra. Your problem, perhaps, will be how to close a simple talk before a group of social workers. How shall you set about it? Let us search a bit. Let us see if we cannot uncover some fertile suggestions.

Summarize Your Points

Even in a short talk of three to five minutes a speaker is very apt to cover so much ground that at the close the listeners are a little hazy about all his main points. However, few speakers realize that. They are misled into assuming that because these points are crystal clear in their own minds, they must be equally lucid to their hearers. Not at all. The speaker has been pondering over his ideas for some time. But his points are all new to the audience; they are flung at the audience like a handful of shot. Some may stick, but the most are liable to roll off in confusion. The hearers are liable, like Iago, to "remember a mass of things but nothing distinctly."

Some anonymous Irish politician is reported to have given this recipe for making a speech: "First, tell them that you are going to tell them; then tell them; then tell them that you have told them." Not bad, you know. In fact, it is often highly advisable to "tell them that you have told them." Briefly, of course, speedily—a mere outline, a summary.

Here is a good example. The speaker was a traffic manager for one of Chicago's railways:

> In short, gentlemen, our own back dooryard experience with this block device, the experience in its use in the East, in the West, in the North—the sound operating principles underlying its operation, the actual demonstration in the money saved in one year in wreck prevention, move me most earnestly and unequivocally to recommend its immediate installation on our Southern branch.

You see what he has done? You can see it and feel it without having heard the rest of the talk. He has summed up in a few sentences, in sixty-two words, practically all the points he has made in the entire talk.

Don't you feel that a summary like that helps? If so, make that technique your own.

Appeal for Action

The closing just quoted is an excellent illustration of the appeal-for-action ending. The speaker wanted something done: a block device installed on the Southern branch of his road. He based his appeal for it on the money it would save, on the wrecks it would prevent. The speaker wanted action, and he got it. This was not a mere practice talk. It was delivered before the board of directors of a certain railway, and it secured the installation of the block device for which it asked.

A Terse, Sincere Compliment

> The great state of Pennsylvania should lead the way in hastening the coming of the new day. Pennsylvania, the great producer of iron and steel, mother of the greatest railroad company in the world, third among our agricultural states—Pennsylvania is the keystone of our business arch. Never was the prospect before her greater, never was her opportunity for leadership more brilliant.

With these words, Charles Schwab closed his address before the Pennsylvania Society of New York. He left his hearers pleased, happy, optimistic. That is an admirable way to finish; but, in order to be effective, it must be sincere. No gross flattery. No extravagances. This kind of closing, if it does not ring true, will ring false, very false. And like a false coin, people will have none of it.

A Humorous Close

"Always leave them laughing," said George Cohan, "when you say good-by." If you have the ability to do it, and the material, fine! But how? That, as Hamlet said, is the question. Each man must do it in his own individual way.

One would hardly expect Lloyd George to leave a gathering of Methodists laughing when he was talking to them on the ultrasolemn subject of John Wesley's Tomb; but note how cleverly he managed it. Note, also, how smoothly and beautifully the talk is rounded off:

> I am glad you have taken in hand the repair of his tomb. It should be honored. He was a man who had a special abhorrence of any absence of neatness or cleanliness. He it was, I think, who said, "Let no one ever see a ragged Methodist." It is due to him that you never can see one. (Laughter.) It is a double unkindness to leave his tomb ragged. You remember what he said to a Derbyshire girl who ran to the door as he was passing and cried, "God bless you, Mr. Wesley." "Young woman," he answered, "your blessing would be of more value if your face and apron were cleaner." (Laughter.) That was his feeling about untidiness. Do not leave his grave untidy. If he passed along, that would hurt him more than anything. Do look after that. It is a memorable and sacred shrine. It is your trust. (Cheers.)

Closing with a Poetical Quotation

Of all methods of ending, none are more acceptable, when well done, than humor or poetry. In fact, if you can get the proper verse of poetry for your closing, it is almost ideal. It will give the desired flavor. It will give dignity. It will give individuality. It will give beauty.

Rotarian Sir Harry Lauder closed his address to the American Rotarian delegates at their Edinburgh convention in this fashion:

> And when you get back home, some of you send me a postcard. I will send you one if you do not send me one. You will easily know it is from me because

there will be no stamp on it. (Laughter.) But I will have some writing on it, and the writing will be this:

"Seasons may come and seasons may go,
Everything withers in due course, you know,
But there is one thing still blooms as fresh as the dew,
That is the love and affection I still have for you."

That little verse fits Harry Lauder's personality, and no doubt it fitted the whole tenor of his talk. Therefore, it was excellent for him. Had some formal and restrained Rotarian used it at the end of a solemn talk, it might have been so out of key as to be almost ridiculous. The longer I teach public speaking, the more clearly I see, the more vividly I feel, that it is impossible to give general rules that will serve on all occasions. So much depends upon the subject, the time, the place, and the man. Everyone must, as Saint Paul said, "work out his own salvation."

I was a guest at a farewell dinner given in honor of the departure of a certain professional man from New York City. A dozen speakers stood up in turn, eulogizing their departing friend, wishing him success in his new field of activity. A dozen talks, and only one ended in an unforgettable manner. That was one that closed with a poetical quotation. The speaker, with emotion in his voice, turned directly to the departing guest, crying: "And now, good-by. Good luck. I wish you every good wish that you can wish yourself!

I touch my heart as the Easterns do:
May the peace of Allah abide with you.
Wherever you come, wherever you go,
May the beautiful palms of Allah grow.
Through days of labor and nights of rest,
May the love of Allah make you blest.
I touch my heart as the Easterns do:
May the peace of Allah abide with you."

Mr. J. A. Abbott, Vice President of the L. A. D. Motors Corporation of Brooklyn, spoke to the employes of his organization on the subject of Loyalty and Coöperation. He closed his address with the ringing verse from Kipling's *Second Jungle Book:*

> Now this is the Law of the Jungle—as old and as true as the sky;
> And the Wolf that shall keep it may prosper, but the Wolf that shall break it must die.
> As the creeper that girdles the tree-trunk, the Law runneth forward and back—
> For the strength of the Pack is the Wolf, and the strength of the Wolf is the Pack.

If you will go to the public library in your town and tell the librarian that you are preparing a talk on a certain subject and that you wish a poetical quotation to express this idea or that, she may be able to help you find something suitable in some reference volume such as Bartlett's Familiar Quotations.

The Power of a Biblical Quotation

If you can quote a passage from Holy Writ to back up your speech, you are fortunate. A choice biblical quotation often has a profound effect. The well-known financier, Frank Vanderlip, used this method in ending his address on the Allied Debts to the United States:

> If we insist to the letter upon our claim, our claim will in all probability never be met. If we insist upon it selfishly, we realize in hatreds but not in cash. If we are generous, and wisely generous, those claims can all be paid, and the good we do with them will mean more to us materially than anything we would conceivably be parting with. "For whosoever will save his life shall lose it; but whosoever shall lose his life for my sake and the gospel's, the same shall save it."

The Climax

The climax is a popular way of ending. It is often difficult to manage and is not an ending for all speakers nor for all subjects. But, when well done, it is excellent. It works up to a crest, a peak, getting stronger sentence by sentence. A good illustration of the climax will be found in the close of the prize-winning speech on Philadelphia in Chapter III.

Lincoln used the climax in preparing his notes for a lecture on Niagara Falls. Note how each comparison is stronger than the preceding, how he gets a cumulative effect by comparing its age to Columbus, Christ, Moses, Adam, and so on:

> It calls up the indefinite past. When Columbus first sought this continent—when Christ suffered on the cross—when Moses led Israel through the Red Sea—nay, even when Adam first came from the hands of his Maker; then, as now, Niagara was roaring here. The eyes of that species of extinct giants whose bones fill the mounds of America have gazed on Niagara, as ours do now. Contemporary with the first race of men, and older than the first man, Niagara is as strong and fresh to-day as ten thousand years ago. The Mammoth and Mastodon, so long dead that fragments of their monstrous bones alone testify that they ever lived, have gazed on Niagara—in that long, long time never still for a moment, never dried, never frozen, never slept, never rested.

Wendell Phillips employed this selfsame technique in his address on Toussaint L'Ouverture. The close of it is quoted below. This selection is often cited in books on public speaking. It has vigor, vitality. It is interesting even though it is a bit too ornate for this practical age. This speech was written more than half a century ago. Amusing, isn't it, to note how woefully wrong were Wendell Phillips' prognostications concerning the historical significance of John Brown and Toussaint L'Ouverture "fifty years hence when truth gets a hearing"? It is as hard evidently to guess history as it is to foretell next year's stock market or the price of lard.

I would call him Napoleon, but Napoleon made his way to empire over broken oaths and through a sea of blood. This man never broke his word. "No Retaliation" was his great motto and the rule of his life; and the last words uttered to his son in France were these: "My boy, you will one day go back to Santo Domingo, forget that France murdered your father." I would call him Cromwell, but Cromwell was only a soldier, and the state he founded went down with him into his grave. I would call him Washington, but the great Virginian held slaves. This man risked his empire rather than permit the slave-trade in the humblest village of his dominions.

You think me a fanatic to-night, for you read history, not with your eyes, but with your prejudices. But fifty years hence, when Truth gets a hearing, the Muse of History will put Phocion for the Greek, and Brutus for the Roman, Hampden for England, Lafayette for France, choose Washington as the bright, consummate flower of our earlier civilization, and John Brown the ripe fruit of our noonday, then, dipping her pen in the sunlight, will write in the clear blue, above them all, the name of the soldier, the statesman, the martyr, Toussaint L'Ouverture.

When the Toe Touches

Hunt, search, experiment until you get a good ending and a good beginning. Then get them close together.

The speaker who does not cut his talk to fit in with the prevailing mood of this hurried, rapid age will be unwelcome and, sometimes, positively disliked.

No less a saint than Saul of Tarsus sinned in this respect. He preached until a chap in the audience, "a young man named Eutychus," went to sleep and fell out of a window and all but broke his neck. Even then Saul may not have stopped talking. Who knows? I remember a speaker, a doctor, standing up one night at the University Club, Brooklyn. It had been a long banquet. Many speakers had already talked. It was two o'clock in the morning when his turn came. Had he been endowed with tact and fine feeling and discretion, he would have said half a dozen sentences and let us go home. But did he? No, not he. He launched into a forty-five minute tirade against vivisection. Long before he was half way through, his audience were wishing that he, like Eutychus, would fall out of a window and break something, anything, to silence him.

Mr. Lorimer, when editor of the *Saturday Evening Post,* told me that he always stopped a series of articles in the *Post* when they were at the height of their popularity, and people were clamoring for more. Why stop then? Why then of all times? "Because," said Mr. Lorimer, "the point of satiation is reached very soon after that peak of popularity."

The same wisdom will apply, and ought to be applied, to speaking. Stop while the audience is still eager to have you go on.

The greatest speech Christ ever delivered, the Sermon on the Mount, can be repeated in five minutes. Lincoln's Gettysburg address has only ten sentences. One can read the whole story of creation in Genesis in less time than it takes to peruse a murder story in the morning paper. . . . Be brief! Be brief!

Doctor Johnson, Archdeacon of Nyasa, wrote a book about the primitive peoples of Africa. He lived among them, observed them, for forty-nine years. He relates that when a speaker talks too long at a village gathering, or the Gwangwara, the audience silences him with shouts of "Imetosha!" "Imetosha!"—"Enough!" "Enough!"

Another tribe is said to permit a speaker to hold forth only so long as he can stand on one foot. When the toe of the lifted member touches the ground, *finito*. He has come to an end.

And the average audience, even though they may be

more polite, more restrained, dislike long speeches just as much.

So be warned by their lot,
Which I know you will not,
And learn about speaking from them.

Summary

1. The close of a speech is really its most strategic element. What is said last is likely to be remembered longest.

2. Do not end with: "That is about all I have to say on the matter; so I guess I will stop." Stop, but don't talk about stopping.

3. Plan your ending carefully in advance as Webster, Bright, and Gladstone did. Rehearse. Know almost word for word how you are going to close. Round off your talk. Don't leave it rough and broken like a jagged rock.

4. Seven suggested ways of closing:

   a. Summarizing, restating, outlining briefly the main points you have covered.

   b. Appealing for action.

   c. Paying the audience a sincere compliment.

   d. Raising a laugh.

   e. Quoting a fitting verse of poetry.

   f. Using a biblical quotation.

   g. Building up a climax.

5. Get a good ending and a good beginning; and get them close together. Always stop before your audience wants you to. "The point of satiation is reached very soon after the peak of popularity."

CHAPTER TEN

How to Make Your Meaning Clear

A famous English bishop, during World War I, spoke to some unlettered troops at Camp Upton. They were on their way to the trenches; but a very small percentage of them had any adequate idea why they were being sent. I know: I questioned them. Yet the Lord Bishop talked to these men about "international amity," and "Serbia's right to a place in the sun." Why, the half of them did not know whether Serbia was a town or a disease. He might as well, as far as results were concerned, have delivered a sonorous eulogy on the Nebular Hypothesis. However, not a single trooper left the hall while he was speaking: the military police with revolvers were stationed at every exit to prevent it.

I do not wish to belittle the bishop. Before a body of collegiate men he would probably have been powerful; but he failed with these soldiers, and he failed utterly: he did not know his audience, and he evidently knew neither the precise purpose of his talk nor how to accomplish it.

What do we mean by the purpose of an address? Just this: every talk, regardless of whether the speaker realizes it or not, has one of four major goals. What are they?

1. To make something clear.
2. To impress and convince.
3. To get action.
4. To entertain.

Let us illustrate these by a series of concrete examples.

Lincoln, who was always more or less interested in mechanics, once invented and patented a device for lifting stranded boats off sand bars and other obstructions. He worked in a mechanic's shop near his law office, making a model of his apparatus. Although the device finally came to naught, he was decidedly enthusiastic over its possibilities. When friends came to his office to view the model, he took no end of pains to explain it. The main purpose of those explanations was clearness.

When he delivered his immortal oration at Gettysburg, when he gave his first and second inaugural addresses, when Henry Clay died and Lincoln delivered a eulogy on his life—on all these occasions, Lincoln's main purpose was impressiveness and conviction. He had to be clear, of course, before he could be convincing; but, in these instances, clearness was not his major consideration.

In his talks to juries, he tried to win favorable decisions. In his political talks, he tried to win votes. His purpose, then, was *action.*

Two years before he was elected President, Lincoln prepared a lecture on Inventions. His purpose was entertainment. At least, that should have been his goal; but he was evidently not very successful in attaining it. His career as a popular lecturer was, in fact, a distinct disappointment. In one town, not a person came to hear him.

But he did succeed and he succeeded famously in the other speeches of his that I have referred to. And why? Because, in those instances, he knew his goal, and he knew how to achieve it. He knew where he wanted to go and how to get there. And because so many speakers don't know just that, they often flounder and come to grief.

For example: I once saw a United States Congressman

hooted and hissed and forced to leave the stage of the old New York Hippodrome, because he had—unconsciously, no doubt, but nevertheless, unwisely—chosen clearness as his goal. It was during the war. He talked to his audience about how the United States was preparing. The crowd did not want to be instructed. They wanted to be entertained. They listened to him patiently, politely, for ten minutes, a quarter of an hour, hoping the performances would come to a rapid end. But it didn't. He rambled on and on; patience snapped; the audience would not stand for more. Someone began to cheer ironically. Others took it up. In a moment, a thousand people were whistling and shouting. The speaker, obtuse and incapable as he was of sensing the temper of his audience, had the bad taste to continue. That aroused them. A battle was on. Their impatience mounted to ire. They determined to silence him. Louder and louder grew their storm of protest. Finally, the roar of it, the anger of it drowned his words—he could not have been heard twenty feet away. So he was forced to give up, acknowledge defeat, and retire in humiliation.

Profit by his example. Know your goal. Choose it wisely before you set out to prepare your talk. Know how to reach it. Then set about it, doing it skillfully and with science.

Use Comparisons to Promote Clearness

As to clearness: do not underestimate the importance of it or the difficulty. I once heard a certain Irish poet give an evening of readings from his own poems. Not ten per cent of the audience, half the time, knew what he was talking about. Many talkers, both in public and private, are a lot like that.

When I discussed the essentials of public speaking with Sir Oliver Lodge, a man who had been lecturing to university classes and to the public for forty years, he emphasized most of all the importance, first, of knowledge and preparation; second, of "taking good pains to be clear."

General Von Moltke, at the outbreak of the Franco-Prussian War, said to his officers: "Remember, gentlemen, that any order that *can* be misunderstood, *will* be misunderstood."

Napoleon recognized the same danger. His most emphatic and oft-reiterated instruction to his secretaries was: "Be clear! Be clear!"

When the disciples asked Christ why he taught the public by parables, he answered: "Because they seeing, see not: and hearing, hear not; neither do they understand."

And when you talk on a subject strange to your hearer or hearers, can you hope that they will understand you any more readily than people understood the Master?

Hardly. So what can we do about it? What did he do when confronted by a similar situation? Solved it in the most simple and natural manner imaginable: described the things people did not know by likening them to things they did know. The kingdom of Heaven . . . what would it be like? How could those untutored peasants of Palestine know? So Christ described it in terms of objects and actions with which they were already familiar:

> The kingdom of Heaven is like unto leaven, which a woman took, and hid in three measures of meal, till the whole was leavened.
>
> Again, the kingdom of Heaven is like unto a merchantman seeking goodly pearls. . . .
>
> Again, the kingdom of Heaven is like unto a net that was cast into the sea. . . .

That was lucid; they could understand that. The housewives in the audience were using leaven every week; the fishermen were casting their nets into the sea daily; the merchants were dealing in pearls.

And how did David make clear the watchfulness and loving kindness of Jehovah?

> The Lord is my shepherd, I shall not want. He maketh me to lie down in green pastures, He leadeth me beside the still waters. . . .

Green grazing grounds in that almost barren country . . . still waters where the sheep could drink—those pastoral people could understand that.

Here is a rather striking and half-amusing example of the use of this principle: some missionaries were translating the Bible into the dialect of a tribe living near equatorial Africa. They progressed to the verse: "Though your sins be as scarlet, they shall be white as snow." How were they to translate that? Literally? Meaningless. Absurd. The natives had never scooped off the sidewalk on a February morning. They did not even have a word for snow. They could not have told the difference between snow and coal tar; but they had climbed cocoanut trees many times and shaken down a few nuts for lunch; so the missionaries likened the unknown to the known, and changed the verse to read: "Though your sins be as scarlet, they shall be as white as the meat of a cocoanut."

Under the circumstances, it would be hard to improve on that, wouldn't it?

At the State Teachers' College at Warrensburg, Missouri, I once heard a lecturer on Alaska who failed, in many places, to be either clear or interesting because, unlike those African missionaries, he neglected to talk in terms of what his audience knew. He told us, for example, that Alaska had a gross area of 590,804 square miles, and a population of 64,356.

Half a million square miles—what does that mean to the average man? Precious little. He is not used to thinking in terms of square miles. They conjure up no mental picture. He does not have any idea whether half a million square miles are approximately the size of Maine or Texas. Suppose the speaker had said that the coast line of Alaska and its islands is longer than the distance around the globe, and that its area more than equals the combined areas of Vermont, New Hampshire, Maine, Massachusetts, Rhode Island, Connecticut, New York, New Jersey, Pennsylvania, Delaware, Maryland, West Virginia, North Carolina, South Carolina, Georgia, Florida, Mississippi and Tennessee.

Would not that give everyone a fairly clear conception of the area of Alaska?

He said the population was 64,356. The chances are that not one person in ten remembered the census figures for five minutes—or even one minute. Why? Because the rapid saying of "sixty-four thousand, three hundred and fifty-six" does not make a very clear impression. It leaves only a loose, insecure impression, like words written on the sand of the seashore. The next wave of attention quite obliterates them. Would it not have been better to have stated the census in terms of something with which they were very familiar? For example: St. Joseph was not very far away from that little Missouri town where the audience lived. Many of them had been to St. Joseph; and, Alaska had, at that time, ten thousand fewer people than St. Joseph. Better still, why not talk about Alaska in terms of the very town where you are speaking? Wouldn't the speaker have been far clearer had he said: "Alaska is eight times as large as the state of Missouri; yet it has only thirteen times as many people as live right here in Warrensburg"?

In the following illustrations, which are the clearer, the *a* statement or the *b?*

(a) Our nearest star is thirty-five trillion miles away.

(b) A train going at the rate of a mile a minute would reach our nearest star in forty-eight million years; if a song were sung there and the sound could travel here it would be three million, eight hundred thousand years before we could hear it. A spider's thread reaching to it would weigh five hundred tons.

(a) St. Peter's, the biggest church in the world, is 232 yards long, and 364 feet wide.

(b) It is about the size of two buildings like the Capitol at Washington piled on top of one another.

Sir Oliver Lodge happily used this method when explaining the size and nature of atoms to a popular audience. I heard him tell a European audience that there were as many atoms in a drop of water as there were drops of water in the Mediterranean Sea; and many of his hearers had spent over a week sailing from Gibraltar to the Suez Canal. To bring the matter still closer home, he said there were as many atoms in one drop of water as there were blades of grass on all the earth.

Richard Harding Davis told a New York audience that the Mosque of St. Sophia was "about as big as the auditorium of the Fifth Avenue theater." He said Brindisi "looks like Long Island City when you come into it from the rear."

Use this principle henceforth in your talks. If you are describing the great pyramid, first tell your hearers it is 451 feet, then tell them how high that is in terms of some building they see every day. Tell how many city blocks the base would cover. Don't speak about so many thousand gallons of this or so many hundred thousand barrels of that without also telling how many rooms the size of the one you are speaking in could be filled with that much liquid. Instead of saying twenty feet high, why not say one and a half times as high as this ceiling. Instead of talking about distance in terms of rods or miles, is it not clearer to say as far as from here to the union station, or to such and such a street?

Avoid Technical Terms

If you belong to a profession the work of which is technical—if you are a lawyer, a physician, an engineer, or are in a highly specialized line of business—be doubly careful when you talk to outsiders, to express yourself in plain terms and to give necessary details.

I say be doubly careful, for, as a part of my professional duties, I have listened to hundreds of speeches that failed right at this point and failed woefully. The speakers appeared totally unconscious of the general public's widespread and profound ignorance regarding their particular specialties. So what happened? They rambled on and on, uttering thoughts, using phrases that fitted into their experience and were instantly and continuously meaningful to them; but to the uninitiated, they were about as clear as the Mississippi River after the June rains have fallen on the newly-plowed corn fields of Iowa and Kansas.

What should such a speaker do? He ought to read and heed the following advice from the facile pen of ex-Senator Beveridge of Indiana:

> It is a good practice to pick out the least intelligent looking person in the audience and strive to make that person interested in your argument. This can be done only by lucid statement of fact and clear reasoning. An even better method is to center your talk on some small boy or girl present with parents.
>
> Say to yourself—say out loud to your audience, if you like—that you will try to be so plain that the child will understand and remember your explanation of the question discussed, and after the meeting be able to tell what you have said.

I remember hearing a physician remark in the course of his talk that "diaphragmatic breathing is a distinct aid to the peristaltic action of the intestines and a boon to health." He was about to dismiss that phase of his talk with that one sentence and to rush on to something else. I stopped him; and asked for a show of hands of those who had a clear conception of how diaphragmatic breathing differs from other kinds of breathing, why it is especially beneficial to physical well-being and what peristaltic action is. The result of the vote surprised the doctor; so he went back, explained, enlarged in this fashion:

> The diaphragm is a thin muscle forming the floor of the chest at the base of the lungs and the roof of the abdominal cavity. When inactive and during chest breathing, it is arched like an inverted washbowl.
>
> In abdominal breathing every breath forces this muscular arch down until it becomes nearly flat and you

can feel your stomach muscles pressing against your belt. This downward pressure of the diaphragm massages and stimulates the organs of the upper part of the abdominal cavity—the stomach, the liver, the pancreas, the spleen, the solar plexus.

When you breathe out again, your stomach and your intestines will be forced up against the diaphragm and will be given another massage. This massaging helps the process of elimination.

A vast amount of ill health originates in the intestines. Most indigestion, constipation, and auto-intoxication would disappear if our stomachs and intestines were properly exercised through deep diaphragmatic breathing.

The Secret of Lincoln's Clearness

Lincoln had a deep and abiding affection for putting a proposition so that it would be instantly clear to everyone. In his first message to Congress, he used the phrase "sugar-coated." Mr. Defrees, the public printer, being Lincoln's personal friend, suggested to him that although the phrase might be all right for a stump speech in Illinois, it was not dignified enough for a historical state paper. "Well, Defrees," Lincoln replied, "if you think the time will ever come when the people will not understand what 'sugar-coated' means, I'll alter it; otherwise, I think I'll let it go."

He once explained to Dr. Gulliver, the president of Knox College, how he developed his "passion" for plain language, as he phrased it:

> Among my earliest recollections I remember how, when a mere child, I used to get irritated when anybody talked to me in a way I could not understand. I don't think I ever got angry at anything else in my life. But that always disturbed my temper, and has ever since. I can remember going to my little bedroom, after hearing the neighbors talk of an evening with my father, and

spending no small part of the night walking up and down and trying to make out the exact meaning of some of their, to me, dark sayings. I could not sleep, though I often tried to, when I got on such a hunt after an idea, until I had caught it, and when I thought I had got it I was not satisfied until I had repeated it over and over, until I had put it in language plain enough as I thought for any boy I knew to comprehend. This was a kind of passion with me, and it has since stuck by me.

A passion? Yes, it must have amounted to that, for Mentor Graham, the schoolmaster of New Salem, testified: "I have known Lincoln to study for hours the best way of three to express an idea."

An all too common reason why people fail to be intelligible is this: the thing they wish to express is not clear even to themselves. Hazy impressions! Indistinct, vague ideas! The result? Their minds work no better in a mental fog than a camera does in a physical fog. They need to be as disturbed over obscurity and ambiguity as Lincoln was. They need to use his methods.

Appeal to the Sense of Sight

The nerves that lead from the eye to the brain are, as we observed in Chapter IV, many times larger than those leading from the ear; and science tells us that we give twenty-five times as much attention to eye suggestions as we do to ear suggestions.

"One seeing," says an old Chinese proverb, "is better than a hundred times telling about."

So, if you wish to be clear, picture your points, visualize your ideas. That was the plan of the late John H. Patterson, president of the well-known National Cash Register Company. He wrote an article for *System Magazine,* outlining the methods he used in speaking to his workmen and his sales forces:

I hold that one cannot rely on speech alone to make

himself understood or to gain and hold attention. A dramatic supplement is needed. It is better to supplement whenever possible with pictures which show the right and the wrong way; diagrams are more convincing than mere words, and pictures are more convincing than diagrams. The ideal presentation of a subject is one in which every subdivision is pictured and in which the words are used only to connect them. I early found that in dealing with men, a picture was worth more than anything I could say.

Little grotesque drawings are wonderfully effective. . . . I have a whole system of cartooning or "chart talks." A circle with a dollar mark means a piece of money, a bag marked with a dollar is a lot of money. Many good effects can be had with moon faces. Draw a circle, put in a few dashes for the eyes, nose, mouth, and ears. Twisting these lines gives the expressions. The out-of-date man has the corner of his mouth down; the chipper, up-to-date fellow has the curves up. The drawings are homely, but the most effective cartoonists are not the men who make the prettiest pictures; the thing is to express the idea and the contrast.

The big bag and the little bag of money, side by side, are the natural heads for the right way as opposed to the wrong way; the one brings much money, the other little money. If you sketch these rapidly as you talk, there is no danger of people's letting their minds wander; they are bound to look at what you are doing and thus to go with you through the successive stages to the point you want to make. And again, the funny figures put people in good humor.

I used to employ an artist to hang around in the shops with me and quietly make sketches of things that were not being done right. Then the sketches were made into drawings and I called the men together and showed them exactly what they were doing. When I heard of the stereopticon I immediately bought one and projected the drawings on the screen, which, of course, made them even more effective than on paper. Then came the moving picture. I think that I had one of the first machines ever made and now we have a big department with many motion picture films and more than 60,000 colored stereopticon slides.

Not every subject or occasion, of course, lends itself to exhibits and drawings; but let us use them when we can. They attract attention, stimulate interest and often make our meaning doubly clear.

Rockefeller Raking Off the Coins

Mr. Rockefeller also used the columns of *System Magazine* to tell how he appealed to the sense of sight to make clear the financial situation of the Colorado Fuel and Iron Company:

> I found that they (the employees of the Colorado Fuel and Iron Co.) imagined the Rockefellers had been drawing immense profits from their interests in Colorado; no end of people had told them so. I explained the exact situation to them. I showed them that during the fourteen years in which we had been connected with the Colorado Fuel and Iron Co., it had never paid one cent of dividends upon the common stock.
>
> At one of our meetings, I gave a practical illustration of the finances of the company. I put a number of coins on the table. I swept off a portion which represented their wages—for the first claim upon the company is the pay roll. Then I took away more coins to represent the salaries of the officers, and then the remaining coins to represent the fees of the directors. There were no coins left for the stockholders. And when I asked: "Men, is it fair, in this corporation where we are all partners, that three of the partners should get all the earnings, be they large or small—all of them—and the fourth nothing?"

Make your eye appeals definite and specific. Paint mental pictures that stand out as sharp and clear as a stag's horn silhouetted against the setting sun. For example, the word "dog" calls up a more or less definite picture of such an animal—perhaps a cocker spaniel, a Scotch terrier, a St. Bernard, or a Pomeranian. Notice how much more distinct an image springs into your mind when I say "bulldog"—the term is less inclusive. Doesn't "a brindle bulldog" call up a still more explicit picture? Is it not more vivid to say "a black Shetland pony" than to talk of "a horse"? Doesn't "a white bantam rooster with a broken leg" give a much more definite and sharp picture than merely the word "fowl"?

Restate Your Important Ideas in Different Words

Napoleon declared repetition to be the only serious principle of rhetoric. He knew that because an idea was clear to him was not always proof that it was instantly grasped by others. He knew that it takes time to comprehend new ideas, that the mind must be kept focused on them. In short, he knew they must be repeated. Not in exactly the same language. People will rebel at that, and rightly so. But if the repetition is couched in fresh phraseology, if it is varied, your hearers will never regard it as repetition at all.

Let us take a specific example. The late Mr. Bryan said:

> You cannot make people understand a subject, unless you understand that subject yourself. The more clearly you have a subject in mind, the more clearly can you present that subject to the minds of others.

The last sentence here is merely a restatement of the idea contained in the first; but when these sentences are spoken, the mind does not have time to see that it is repetition. It only *feels* that the subject has been made more clear.

I seldom teach a single session of my courses without hearing one or perhaps half a dozen talks that would have been more clear, more impressive, had the speaker but employed this principle of restatement. It is almost entirely ignored by the beginner. And what a pity!

Use General Illustrations and Specific Instances

One of the surest and easiest ways to make your points clear is to follow them with general illustrations and concrete cases. What is the difference between the two? One, as the term implies, is general; the other, specific.

Let us illustrate the difference between them and the uses of each with a concrete example. Suppose we take the statement: "There are professional men and women who earn astonishingly large incomes."

Is that statement very clear? Have you a clear-cut idea of what the speaker really means? No, and the speaker himself cannot be sure of what such an assertion will call up in the minds of others. It may cause the country doctor in the Ozark Mountains to think of a family doctor in a small city with an income of five thousand. It may cause a successful mining engineer to think in terms of the men in his profession who make a hundred thousand a year. The statement, as it stands, is entirely too vague and loose. It needs to be tightened. A few illuminating details ought to be given to indicate what professions the speaker refers to and what he means by "astonishingly large."

> There are lawyers, prize fighters, song writers, novelists, playwrights, painters, actors and singers who make more than the President of the United States.

Now, hasn't one a much clearer idea of what the speaker meant? However, he has not individualized. He has used general illustrations, not specific instances. He has said "singers," not Rosa Ponselle, Kirsten Flagstad, or Lily Pons.

So the statement is still more or less vague. We cannot call up concrete cases to illustrate it. Should not the speaker do it for us? Would he not be clearer if he employed specific examples—as is done in the following paragraph?

> The great trial lawyers Samuel Untermeyer and Max Steuer earn as much as one million dollars a year. Jack

Dempsey's annual income has been known to bc as high as a half million dollars. Joe Louis, the young, uneducated Negro pugilist, while still in his twenties, earned more than a half million dollars. Irving Berlin's ragtime music is reported to have brought him a half million dollars yearly. Sidney Kingsley made ten thousand dollars a week royalty on his plays. H. G. Wells admitted, in his autobiography, that his pen had brought him three million dollars. Diego Rivera earned, from his paintings, more than a half a million dollars in a year. Katharine Cornell has repeatedly refused five thousand dollars a week to go into pictures.

Now, has not one an extremely plain and vivid idea of exactly and precisely what the speaker wanted to convey?

Be concrete. Be definite. Be specific. This quality of definiteness not only makes for clearness but for impressiveness and conviction and interest also.

Do Not Emulate the Mountain Goat

Professor William James, in one of his talks to teachers, paused to remark that one can make only one point in a lecture, and the lecture he referred to lasted an hour. Yet I recently heard a speaker, who was limited by a stop watch to three minutes, begin by saying that he wanted to call our attention to eleven points. Sixteen and a half seconds to each phase of his subject! Seems incredible, doesn't it, that an intelligent man should attempt anything so manifestly absurd. True, I am quoting an extreme case; but the tendency to err in that fashion, if not to that degree, handicaps almost every novice. He is like a Cook's guide who shows Paris to the tourist in one day. It can be done, just as one can walk through the American Museum of Natural History in thirty minutes. But neither clearness nor enjoyment results. Many a talk fails to be clear because the speaker seems intent upon establishing a world's record for ground covered in the allotted time. He leaps from one point to another with the swiftness and agility of a mountain goat.

Most talks must be short, so cut your cloth accordingly. If, for example, you are to speak on Labor Unions, do not attempt to tell in three or six minutes why they came into existence, the methods they employ, the good they have accomplished, the evil they have wrought, and how to solve industrial disputes. No, no; if you strive to do that, no one will have a very clear conception of what you have said. It will be all confused, a blur, too sketchy, too much of a mere outline.

Wouldn't it be the part of wisdom to take one phase and one phase only of labor unions, and cover that adequately and illustrate it? It would. That kind of speech leaves a single impression. It is lucid, easy to listen to, easy to remember.

However, if you must cover several phases of your topic, it is often advisable to summarize briefly at the end. Let us see how that suggestion operates. Here is a summary of this lesson. Does the reading of it help to make the message we have been presenting more lucid, more comprehensible?

Summary

1. To be clear is highly important and often very difficult. Christ declared that he had to teach by parables, "Because they (his hearers) seeing, see not; and hearing, hear not; neither do they understand."

2. Christ made the unknown clear by talking of it in terms of the known. He likened the kingdom of heaven to leaven, to nets cast into the sea, to merchants buying pearls. "Go thou, and do likewise." If you wish to give a clear conception of the size of Alaska, do not quote its area in square miles; name the states that could be put into it; enumerate its population in terms of the town where you are speaking.

3. Avoid technical terms when addressing a lay audience. Follow Lincoln's plan of putting your ideas into language plain enough for any boy or girl to comprehend.

4. Be sure that the thing you wish to speak about is first as clear as noonday sunshine in your own mind.

5. Appeal to the sense of sight. Use exhibits, pictures, illustrations when possible. Be definite. Don't say "dog" if you mean "a fox terrier with a black splotch over his right eye."

6. Restate your big ideas; but don't repeat, don't use the same phrases twice. Vary the sentences, but reiterate the idea without letting your hearers detect it.

7. Make your abstract statement clear by following it with general illustrations—and what is often better still—by specific instances and concrete cases.

8. Do not strive to cover too many points. In a short

speech, one cannot hope to treat adequately more than one or two phases of a big topic.

9. Close with a brief summary of your points.

CHAPTER ELEVEN

How to Interest Your Audience

This page you are reading now, this sheet of paper you are looking at—it is very ordinary, isn't it? You have seen countless thousands of such pages. It seems dull and insipid now; but if I tell you a strange fact about it, you are almost sure to be interested. Let us see! This page seems like solid matter as you look at it now. But, in reality, it is more like a cobweb than solid matter. The physicist knows it is composed of atoms. And how small is an atom? We learned in Chapter X that there are as many atoms in one drop of water as there are drops of water in the Mediterranean Sea, that there are as many atoms in one drop of water as there are blades of grass in all the world. And the atoms that make this paper are composed of what? Still smaller things called electrons and protons. These electrons are all rotating around the central proton of the atom, as far from it, relatively speaking, as the moon is from the earth. And they are swinging through their orbits, these electrons of this tiny universe, at the inconceivable speed of approximately ten thousand miles a second. So the electrons that compose this sheet of paper you are holding have moved, since you began reading this very sentence, a distance equal to that which stretches between New York and Tokyo. . . .

And only two minutes ago you may have thought this piece of paper was still and dull and dead; but, in reality, it is one of God's mysteries. It is a veritable cyclone of energy.

If you are interested in it now, it is because you have learned a new and strange fact about it. There lies one of the secrets of interesting people. That is a significant truth, one that we ought to profit by in our everyday intercourse. The entirely new is not interesting; the entirely old has no attractiveness for us. We want to be told something new about the old. You cannot, for example, interest an Illinois farmer with a description of the Cathedral at Bourges, or the Mona Lisa. They are too new to him. There is no tie-up to his old interests. But you can interest him by relating the fact that farmers in Holland till land below the level of the sea and dig ditches to act as fences and build bridges to serve as gates. Your Illinois farmer will listen open-mouthed while you tell him that Dutch farmers keep the cows, during the winter, under the same roof that houses the family, and sometimes the cows look out through lace curtains at driving snows. He knows about cows and fences —new slants, you see, on old things. "Lace curtains! For a cow!" he'll exclaim. "I'll be doggoned!" And he will retail that story to his friends.

Here is another talk. As you read it, see if it interests you. If it does, do you know why?

How Sulphuric Acid Affects You

Most liquids are measured by the pint, quart, gallon or barrel. We ordinarily speak of quarts of wine, gallons of milk, and barrels of molasses. When a new oil gusher is discovered, we speak of its output as so many barrels per day. There is one liquid, however, that is manufactured and consumed in such large quantities that the unit of measurement employed is the ton. This liquid is sulphuric acid.

It touches you in your daily life in a score of ways. If it were not for sulphuric acid, your car would stop, and you would go back to "old Dobbin" and the buggy, for it is used extensively in the refining of kerosene and gasoline. The electric lights that illuminate your office, that shine upon your dinner table, that show you the way to bed at night, would not be possible without it.

When you get up in the morning and turn on the water for your bath, you use a nickel-plated faucet, which requires sulphuric acid in its manufacture. It was required also in the finishing of your enameled tub. The soap you use has possibly been made from greases or oils that have been treated with the acid. . . . Your towel has made its acquaintance before you made the acquaintance of your towel. The bristles in your hair-brush have required it, and your celluloid comb could not have been produced without it. Your razor, no doubt, has been pickled in it after annealing.

You put on your underwear; you button up your outer garments. The bleacher, the manufacturer of dyes and the dyer himself used it. The button-maker possibly found the acid necessary to complete your buttons. The tanner used sulphuric acid in making the leather for your shoes, and it serves us again when we wish to polish them.

You come down to breakfast. The cup and saucer, if they be other than plain white, could not have come into being without it. It is used to produce the gilt and other ornamental colorings. Your spoon, knife and fork have seen a bath of sulphuric acid, if they be silver-plated.

The wheat of which your bread or rolls are made has possibly been grown by the use of a phosphate fertilizer, whose manufacture rests upon this acid. If you have buckwheat cakes and syrup, your syrup needed it. . . .

And so on through the whole day, its work affects you at every turn. Go where you will, you cannot escape its influence. We can neither go to war without it nor live in peace without it. So it hardly seems possible that this acid, so essential to mankind, should be totally unfamiliar to the average man. . . . But such is the case.

The Three Most Interesting Things in the World

What would you say they are—the three most interesting subjects in the world? Sex, property and religion. By the first we can create life, by the second we maintain it, by the third we hope to continue it in the world to come.

But it is *our* sex, *our* property, *our* religion that interests us. Our interests swarm about our own egos.

We are not interested in a talk on How to Make Wills in Peru; but we may be interested in a talk entitled: How to Make Our Wills. We are not interested—except, perhaps, out of curiosity—in the religion of the Hindu; but we are vitally interested in a religion that insures *us* unending happiness in the world to come.

When the late Lord Northcliffe was asked what interests people, he answered with one word—and that word was "themselves." Northcliffe ought to have known for he was the wealthiest newspaper owner in Great Britain.

Do you want to know what kind of person you are? Ah, now we are on an interesting topic. We are talking about *you*. Here is a way for *you* to hold the mirror up to your real self, and see *you* as *you* really are. Watch your reveries. What do we mean by reveries? Let Professor James Harvey Robinson answer. We are quoting from *The Mind in the Making:*

> We all appear to ourselves to be thinking all the time during our waking hours, and most of us are aware that we go on thinking while we are asleep, even more foolishly than when awake. When uninterrupted by some practical issue we are engaged in what is now known as a *reverie*. This is our spontaneous and favorite kind of thinking. We allow our ideas to take their own course and this course is determined by our hopes and fears, our spontaneous desires, their fulfillment or frustration; by our likes and dislikes, our loves and hates and resentments. *There is nothing else anything like so interesting to ourselves as ourselves.* All thought that is not more or less laboriously controlled and directed will inevitably

> circle about the beloved Ego. It is amusing and pathetic to observe this tendency in ourselves and in others. We lean politely and generously to overlook this truth, but if we dare to think of it, it blazes forth like the noontide sun.
>
> Our reveries form the chief index of our fundamental character. They are a reflection of our nature as modified by often hidden and forgotten experiences. . . . The reverie doubtless influences all our speculations in its persistent tendency to self-magnification and self-justification, which are its chief preoccupations.

So remember that the people you are to talk to spend most of their time when they are not concerned with the problems of homemaking or case work or business, in thinking about and justifying and glorifying themselves. Remember that the average person will be more concerned about the cook leaving than about Italy paying her debts to the United States. He will be more wrought up over a dull razor blade than over a revolution in South America. A woman's own toothache will distress her more than an earthquake in Asia destroying half a million lives. She would rather listen to you say some nice thing about her than hear you discuss the ten greatest men in history.

How to Be a Good Conversationalist

The reason so many people are poor conversationalists is that they talk about only the things that interest them. That may be deadly boring to others. Reverse the process. Lead the other person into talking about *his* interests, *his* business, *his* golf score, *his* success—or, if it is a mother, *her* children. Do that and listen intently and you will give pleasure; consequently you will be considered a good conversationalist—even though you have done very little of the talking.

Mr. Harold Dwight of Philadelphia made an extraordinarily successful speech at a banquet which marked the final session of a public speaking course. He talked about each man in turn around the entire table, told how he had talked when the course started, how he had improved; recalled the talks various members had made, the subjects they had discussed; he mimicked some of them, exaggerated their peculiarities, had everyone laughing, had everyone pleased. With such material, he could not possibly have failed. It was absolutely ideal. No other topic under the blue dome of heaven would have so interested that group. Mr. Dwight knew how to handle human nature.

An Idea That Won Two Million Readers

Some years ago, the *American Magazine* enjoyed an amazing growth. Its sudden leap in circulation became one of the sensations of the publishing world. The secret? The secret was the late John M. Siddall and his ideas. When I first met Siddall he had charge of the Interesting People Department of that periodical. I had written a few articles for him; and one day he sat down and talked to me for a long time:

"People are selfish," he said. "They are interested chiefly in themselves. They are not very much concerned about whether the government should own the railroads; but they do want to know how to get ahead, how to draw more salary, how to keep healthy. If I were editor of this magazine," he went on, "I would tell them how to take care of their teeth, how to take baths, how to keep cool in summer, how to get a position, how to handle employees, how to buy homes, how to remember, how to avoid grammatical errors, and so on. People are always interested in human stories, so I would have some rich man tell how he made a million in real estate. I would get prominent bankers and presidents of various corporations to tell the stories of how they battled their ways up from the ranks to power and wealth."

Shortly after that, Siddall was made editor. The magazine then had a small circulation, was comparatively a failure. Siddall did just what he said he would do. The response? It was overwhelming. The circulation figures climbed up to two hundred thousand, three, four, half a million. . . . Here was something the public wanted. Soon a million people a month were buying it, then a million and a half, finally two millions. It did not stop there, but continued to grow for many years. Siddall appealed to the selfish interests of his readers.

The Kind of Speech Material That Always Holds Attention

You may possibly bore people if you talk about things and ideas, but you can hardly fail to hold their attention when you talk about people. Tomorrow there will be millions of conversations floating over fences in the backyards of America, over tea tables and dinner tables—and what will be the predominating note in most of them? Personalities. He said this. Mrs. So-and-so did that. I saw her doing this, that and the other. He is making a "killing," and so on.

I have addressed many gatherings of school children in the United States and Canada; and I soon learned by experience that in order to keep them interested I had to tell them stories about people. As soon as I became general and dealt with abstract ideas, Johnny became restless and wiggled in his seat, Tommy made a face at someone, Billy threw something across the aisle.

I once asked a group of American business men in Paris to talk on "How to Succeed." Most of them praised the homely virtues, preached at, lectured to, and bored their hearers. (Incidentally, I recently heard one of the most prominent business men in America make this identical mistake in a radio talk on this identical topic. So do club women and traveling lecturers.)

So I halted this class, and said something like this: "We don't want to be lectured to. No one enjoys that. Remember you must be entertaining or we will pay no attention whatever to what you are saying. Also remember that one of the most interesting things in the world is sublimated, glorified gossip. So tell us the stories of two persons you have known. Tell why one succeeded and why the other failed. We will gladly listen to that, remember it and possibly profit by it. It will also, by the way, be far easier for you to deliver than are these wordy, abstract preachments."

There was a certain member of that course who invariably found it difficult to interest either himself or his audience. This night, however, he seized the human story suggestion; and told us of two of his classmates in college. One of them had been so frugal that he had bought shirts at the different stores in town, and made charts showing which ones laundered best, wore longest and gave the most service per dollar invested. His mind was always on pennies; yet, when he was graduated—it was an engineering college—he had such a high opinion of his own importance that he was not willing to begin at the bottom and work his way up, as the other graduates were doing. Even when the third annual reunion of the class came, he was still making laundry charts of his shirts, while waiting for some extraordinarily good thing to come his way. It never came. A quarter of a century has passed since then, and this man, dissatisfied and soured on life, still holds a minor position.

The speaker then contrasted with this failure the story of one of his classmates who had surpassed all expectations. This particular chap was a good mixer. Everyone liked him. Although he was ambitious to do big things later, he started as a draughtsman. But he was always on the lookout for opportunity. Plans were then being made for the Pan-American Exposition in Buffalo. He knew engineering talent would be needed there; so he resigned from his position in Philadelphia and moved to Buffalo. Through his agreeable personality, he soon won the friendship of a Buffalo man with considerable political influence. The two formed a partnership, and engaged immediately in the contracting business. They did considerable work for the telephone company, and this man was finally taken over by that concern at a large salary. He became a multimillionaire, one of the principal owners of Western Union.

We have recorded here only the bare outline of what the speaker told. He made his talk interesting and illuminating with a score of amusing and human details. . . . He talked on and on—this man who could not ordinarily find material for a three-minute speech—and he was surprised beyond words to learn when he stopped that he had held the floor on this occasion for half an hour. The speech had been so interesting that it seemed short to everyone. It was this student's first real triumph.

Almost everyone can profit by this incident. The average speech would be far more appealing if it were rich and replete with human interest stories. The speaker ought to attempt to make only a few points and to illustrate them with concrete cases. Such a method of speech building can hardly fail to get and hold attention.

If possible, these stories ought to tell of struggles, of things fought for and victories won. All of us are tremendously interested in fights and combats. There is an old saying that all the world loves a lover. It doesn't. What all the world loves is a scrap. It wants to see two lovers struggling for the hand of one woman. As an illustration of this fact, read almost any novel, magazine story, or go to see almost any film drama. When all the obstacles are removed and the reputed hero takes the so-called heroine in his arms, the audience begin reaching for their hats and coats. Five minutes later the sweeping women are gossiping over their broom handles.

Almost all magazine fiction is based on this formula. Make the reader like the hero or heroine. Make him or her long for something intensely. Make that something seem impossible to get. Show how the hero or heroine fights and gets it.

The story of how a man battled in business or profession against discouraging odds, and won, is always inspiring, always interesting. A magazine editor once told me that the real, inside story of any person's life is entertaining. If one has struggled and fought—and who hasn't?—his story, if correctly told, will appeal. There can be no doubt of that.

Be Concrete

The writer once had, in the same course in public speaking, a Doctor of Philosophy and a rough-and-ready fellow who had spent his youth thirty years ago in the British Navy. The polished scholar was a university professor; his classmate from the seven seas was the proprietor of a small side street moving-van establishment. Strange to say, the moving-van man's talks during the course would have held a popular audience far better than the talks of the college professor. Why? The college man spoke in beautiful English, with a demeanor of culture and refinement, and with logic and clearness; but his talks lacked one essential, *concreteness.* They were too vague, too general. On the other hand, the van owner got right down to business immediately. He was definite; he was concrete. That quality, coupled with his virility and his fresh phraseology, made his talks very entertaining.

I have cited this instance, not because it is typical either of college men or moving-van proprietors, but because it illustrates the interest-getting power that accrues to the man—regardless of formal education—who has the happy habit of being concrete and definite in his speaking.

This principle is so important that we are going to use several illustrations to try to lodge it firmly in your mind. We hope you will never forget it, never neglect it.

Is it, for example, more interesting to state that Martin Luther, as a boy, was "stubborn and intractable," or is it better to say that he confessed that his teachers had flogged him as often as "fifteen times in a forenoon"?

Words like "stubborn and intractable" have very little attention value. But isn't it easy to listen to the flogging count?

The old method of writing a biography was to deal in a lot of generalities which Aristotle called, and rightly called, "The refuge of weak minds." The new method is to deal with concrete facts that speak for themselves. The old-fashioned biographer said that John Doe was born of "poor but honest parents." The new method would say that John Doe's father couldn't afford a pair of overshoes, so when the snow came, he had to tie gunny sacking around his shoes to keep his feet dry and warm; but, in spite of his poverty, he never watered the milk and he never traded a horse with the heaves as a sound animal. That shows that his parent were "poor but honest," doesn't it? And doesn't it do it in a way that is far more interesting than the "poor but honest" method?

If this method works for modern biographers it will work also for modern speakers.

Let us take one more illustration. Suppose you wished to state that the potential horse power wasted at Niagara every day was appalling. Suppose you said just that, and then added, that if it were utilized and the resulting profits turned to purchasing the necessities of life, crowds could be clothed and fed. Would that be the way to make it interesting and entertaining? No—no. Isn't this far better? We are quoting from Edwin S. Slosson in the *Daily Science News Bulletin:*

> We are told that there are some millions of people in poverty and poorly nourished in this country, yet here at Niagara is wasted the equivalent of 250,000 loaves of bread an hour. We may see with our mind's eye 600,000 nice fresh eggs dropping over the precipice every hour and making a gigantic omelet in the whirlpool. If calico were continuously pouring from the looms in a stream 4,000 feet wide like Niagara River, it would represent the same destruction of property. If a Carnegie Library were held under the spout it would be filled with good books in an hour or two. Or we can imagine a big department store floating down from Lake Erie every day and smashing its varied contents on the rocks 160 feet below. That would be an exceedingly interesting and diverting spectacle, quite as attractive to the crowd as the present, and no more expensive to maintain. Yet some people might object to that on the ground of extravagance who now object to the utilization of the power of the falling water.

Picture-Building Words

In this process of interest-getting, there is one aid, one technique, that is of the highest importance; yet it is all but ignored. The average speaker does not seem to be aware of its existence. He has probably never consciously thought about it at all. I refer to the process of using words that create pictures. The speaker who is easy to listen to is the one who sets images floating before your eyes. The one who employs foggy, commonplace, colorless symbols sets the audience to nodding.

Pictures. Pictures. Pictures. They are as free as the air you breathe. Sprinkle them through your talks, your conversation; and you will be more entertaining, more influential.

To illustrate: let us take the excerpt just quoted from the *Daily Science News Bulletin* regarding Niagara. Look at the picture words. They leap up and go scampering away in every sentence, as thick as rabbits in Australia: "250,000 loaves of bread, 600,000 eggs dropping over the precipice, gigantic omelet in the whirlpool, calico pouring from the looms in a stream 4,000 feet wide, Carnegie Library held under the spout, books, a big department store floating, smashing, rocks below, falling water."

It would be almost as difficult to ignore such a talk or article as it would be to pay not the slightest attention to the scenes from a film unwinding on the silver screen of the motion picture theater.

Herbert Spencer, in his famous little essay on the *Philosophy of Style,* pointed out long ago the superiority of terms that call forth bright pictures:

> "We do not think," says he, "in generals but in particulars. . . . We should avoid such a sentence as
>
> "In proportion as the manners, customs and amusements of a nation are cruel and barbarous, the regulations of their penal code will be severe.
>
> "And in place of it, we should write:
>
> "In proportion as men delight in battles, bull fights

and combats of gladiators, will they punish by hanging, burning and the rack."

Picture-building phrases swarm through the pages of the Bible and through Shakespeare like bees around a cider mill. For example, a commonplace writer would have said that a certain thing would be superfluous, like trying to improve the perfect. How did Shakespeare express the same thought? With a picture phrase that is immortal: "To gild refined gold, to paint the lily, to throw perfume on the violet."

Did you ever pause to observe that the proverbs that are passed on from generation to generation are almost all visual sayings? "A bird in the hand is worth two in the bush." "It never rains but it pours." "You can lead a horse to water but you can't make him drink." And you will find the same picture element in almost all the similes that have lived for centuries and grown hoary with too much use: "Sly as a fox." "Dead as a door nail." "Flat as a pancake." "Hard as a rock."

Lincoln continually talked in visual terminology. When he became annoyed with the long, complicated, red-tape reports that came to his desk in the White House, he objected to them, not with a colorless phraseology, but with a picture phrase that it is almost impossible to forget. "When I send a man to buy a horse," said he, "I don't want to be told how many hairs the horse has in his tail. I wish only to know his points."

The Interest-Getting Value of Contrasts

Listen to the following condemnation of Charles I by Macaulay. Note that Macaulay not only uses pictures, but he also employs balanced sentences. Violent contrasts almost always hold our interests; violent contrasts are the very brick and mortar of this paragraph:

> We charge him with having broken his coronation oath; and we are told that he kept his marriage vow!

We accuse him of having given up his people to the merciless inflictions of the most hot-headed of prelates; and the defense is that he took his little son on his knee and kissed him! We censure him for having violated the articles of the Petition of Right, after having, for good and valuable consideration, promised to observe them; and we are informed that he was accustomed to hear prayers at six o'clock in the morning! It is to such considerations as these, together with his Vandyke dress, his handsome face and his peaked beard, that he owes, we verily believe, most of his popularity with the present generation.

Interest Is Contagious

We have been discussing so far the kind of material that interests an audience. However, one might mechanically follow all the suggestions made here and speak according to Cocker, and yet be vapid and dull. Catching and holding the interest of people is a delicate thing, a matter of feeling and spirit. It is not like operating a steam engine. No precise rules can be given for it.

Interest, be it remembered, is contagious. Your hearers are almost sure to catch it if you have a bad case of it yourself. A short time ago, a gentleman rose during a session of my course in Baltimore and warned his audience that if the present methods of catching rock fish in Chesapeake Bay were continued the species would become extinct. And in a very few years! He felt his subject. It was important. He was in real earnest about it. Everything about his matter and manner showed that. When he arose to speak, I did not know that there was such an animal as a rock fish in Chesapeake Bay. I imagine that most of the audience shared my lack of knowledge and lack of interest. But before the speaker finished, all of us had caught something of his concern. All of us would probably have been willing to have signed a petition to the legislature to protect the rock fish by law.

I once asked Richard Washburn Child, then American Ambassador to Italy, the secret of his success as an interesting writer. He replied: "I am so excited about life that I cannot keep still. I just have to tell people about it." One cannot keep from being enthralled with a speaker or writer like that.

I heard a speaker in London: after he was through, one of our party, Mr. E. F. Benson, well-known English novelist, remarked that he enjoyed the last part of the talk far more than the first. When I asked him why, he replied: "The speaker himself seemed more interested in the last part, and I always rely on the speaker to supply the enthusiasm and interest."

Everyone does. Remember that.

Summary

1. We are interested in extraordinary facts about ordinary things.

2. Our chief interest is ourselves.

3. The person who leads others to talk about themselves and their interests and listens intently will generally be considered a good conversationalist, even though he does very little talking.

4. Glorified gossip, stories of people, will almost always win and hold attention. The speaker ought to make only a few points and to illustrate them with human interest stories.

5. Be concrete and definite. Do not belong to the "poor-but-honest" school of speakers. Do not merely say that Martin Luther was "stubborn and intractable" as a boy. Announce that fact. Then follow it with the assertion that his teachers flogged him as often as "fifteen times in a forenoon." That makes the general assertion clear, impressive and interesting.

6. Sprinkle your talks with phrases that create pictures, with words that set images floating before your eyes.

7. If possible use balanced sentences and contrasting ideas.

8. Interest is contagious. The audience is sure to catch it if the speaker himself has a bad case of it. But it cannot be won by the mechanical adherence to mere rules.

CHAPTER TWELVE

Improving Your Diction

An Englishman, without employment and without financial reserves, was walking the streets of Philadelphia seeking a position. He entered the office of Mr. Paul Gibbons, a well-known business man of that city, and asked for an interview. Mr. Gibbons looked at the stranger distrustfully. His appearance was emphatically against him. His clothes were shabby and threadbare, and over all of him were written large the unmistakable signs of financial distress. Half out of curiosity, half out of pity, Mr. Gibbons granted the interview. At first, he had intended to listen for only a moment, but the moments grew into minutes, and the minutes mounted into an hour; and the conversation still continued. It ended by Mr. Gibbons telephoning to Mr. Roland Taylor, the Philadelphia manager for Dillon, Read and Company; and Mr. Taylor, one of the leading financiers of that city, invited this stranger to lunch and secured for him a desirable position. How was this man, with the air and outward appearance of failure, able to effect such a prized connection within so short a time?

The secret can be divulged in a single phrase: his command of the English language. He was, in reality, an Oxford man who had come to this country on a business mission which had ended in disaster, leaving him stranded, without funds and without friends. But he spoke his mother tongue with such precision and beauty that his listeners soon forgot his rusty shoes, his frayed coat, his unshaven face. His diction became an immediate passport into the best business circles.

This man's story is somewhat extraordinary, but it illustrates a broad and fundamental truth, namely, that we are judged each day by our speech. Our words reveal our refinements; they tell the discerning listener of the company we have kept; they are the hallmarks of education and culture.

We have only four contacts with the world, you and I. We are evaluated and classified by four things: by what we do, by how we look, by what we say, and by how we say it. Yet many a person blunders through a long lifetime, after he leaves school, without any conscious effort to enrich his stock of words, to master their shades of meaning, to speak with precision and distinction. He comes habitually to use the overworked and exhausted phrases of the office and street. Small wonder that his talk lacks distinction and individuality. Small wonder that he often violates the accepted traditions of pronunciation, and that he sometimes transgresses the very canons of English grammar itself. I have heard even college graduates say "ain't," and "he don't," and "between you and I." And if people with academic degrees gracing their names commit such errors, what can we expect of those whose education has been cut short by the pressure of economic necessity?

Years ago, I stood one afternoon daydreaming in the Coliseum at Rome. A stranger approached me, an English colonial. He introduced himself, and began talking of his experiences in the Eternal City. He had not spoken three minutes until he had said "you was," and "I done." That morning, when he arose, he had polished his shoes and put on spotless linen in order to maintain his own self-respect and to win the respect of those with whom he came in contact; but he had made no attempt whatever to polish his phrases and to speak spotless sentences. He would have been ashamed, for example, of not raising his hat to a woman when he spoke; but he was not ashamed—no, he was not even conscious—of violating the usages of grammar, of offending the ears of discriminating auditors. By his own words, he stood revealed and placed and classified. His woeful use of the English language proclaimed to the world continually and unmistakably that he was not a person of culture.

Dr. Charles W. Eliot, after he had been president of Harvard for a third of a century, declared: "I recognize but one mental acquisition as a necessary part of the education of a lady or gentleman, namely, an accurate and refined use of the mother tongue." This is a significant pronouncement. Ponder over it.

But how, you ask, are we to become intimate with words, to speak them with beauty and accuracy? Fortunately, there is no mystery about the means to be employed, no legerdemain. The method is an open secret. Lincoln used it with amazing success. No other American ever wove words into such comely patterns, or produced with prose such matchless music: "with malice towards none, with charity for all." Was Lincoln, whose father was a shiftless, illiterate carpenter and whose mother was a woman of no extraordinary attainments—was he endowed by nature with this gift for words? There is no evidence to support such an assumption. When he was elected to Congress, he described his education in the official records at Washington, with one adjective: "defective." He had attended school less than twelve months in his entire life. And who had been his mentors? Zachariah Birney and Caleb Hazel in the forests of Kentucky, Azel Dorsey and Andrew Crawford along Pigeon Creek in Indiana—itinerant pedagogues, all of them, drifting from one pioneer settlement to another, eking out an existence wherever a few scholars could be found who were willing to exchange hams and corn and wheat for the three R's. Lincoln had meager assistance, little of uplift or inspiration from them, and little, too, from his daily environment.

The farmers and merchants, the lawyers and litigants with whom he associated in the Eighth Judicial District of Illinois, possessed no magic with words. But Lincoln did not—and this is the significant fact to remember—Lincoln did not squander all his time with his mental equals and inferiors. He made boon companions out of the elite minds, the singers, the poets of the ages. He could repeat from memory whole pages of Burns and Byron and Browning. He wrote a lecture on Burns. He had one copy of Byron's poems for his office and another for his home. The office copy had been used so much that it fell open, whenever it was lifted, to *Don Juan.* Even when he was in the White House and the tragic burdens of the Civil War were sapping his strength and etching deep furrows in his face, he often found time to take a copy of Hood's poems to bed. Sometimes he awoke in the middle of the night and, opening the book, he chanced upon verses that especially stirred or pleased. Getting up, clad only in his nightshirt and slippers, he stole through the halls until he found his secretary and read to him poem after poem. In the White House, he found time to repeat long, memorized passages from Shakespeare, to criticize the actor's reading of them, to give his own individual interpretation. "I have gone over some of Shakespeare's plays," he wrote Hackett, the actor, "perhaps as frequently as any unprofessional reader. Lear, Richard III, Henry VIII, Hamlet, and especially Macbeth. I think nothing equals Macbeth. It is wonderful!"

Lincoln was devoted to verse. Not only did he memorize and repeat it, both in private and public, but he even essayed to write it. He read one of his long poems at his sister's wedding. Later, in middle life, he filled a notebook with his original compositions, but he was so shy about these creations that he never permitted even his closest friends to read them.

"This self-educated man," writes Robinson in his book, *Lincoln as a Man of Letters,* "clothed his mind with the materials of genuine culture. Call it genius or talent, the process of his attainment was that described by Professor Emerton in speaking of the education of Erasmus: 'He was no longer at school, but was simply educating himself by the only pedagogical method which ever yet produced any results anywhere, namely, by the method of his own tireless energy in continuous study and practice.' "

This awkward prioneer, who used to shuck corn and butcher hogs for 31 cents a day on the Pigeon Creek farms of Indiana, delivered, at Gettysburg, one of the most beautiful addresses ever spoken by mortal man. One hundred and seventy thousand men fought there. Seven thousand were killed. Yet Charles Sumner said, shortly after Lincoln's death, that Lincoln's address would live when the memory of the battle was lost, and that the battle would one day be remembered largely because of the speech. Who will doubt the correctness of this prophecy?

Edward Everett spoke for two hours at Gettysburg; all that he said has long since been forgotten. Lincoln spoke for less than two minutes: a photographer attempted to take his picture while delivering the speech, but Lincoln had finished before the primitive camera could be set up and focused.

Lincoln's address has been cast in imperishable bronze and placed in a library at Oxford as an example of what can be done with the English language. It ought to be memorized by every student of public speaking.

> Four score and seven years ago our fathers brought forth on this continent a new nation, conceived in liberty, and dedicated to the proposition that all men are created equal. Now we are engaged in a great civil war, testing whether that nation, or any nation so conceived and so dedicated, can long endure. We are met on a great battlefield of that war. We have come to dedicate a portion of that field as a final resting-place for those who here gave their lives that that nation might live. It is altogether fitting and proper that we should do this. But in a larger sense we cannot dedicate, we cannot consecrate, we cannot hallow this ground. The brave men, living and dead, who struggled here, have consecrated it, far above our poor power to add or detract. The world will little note, nor long remember, what we say here, but it can never forget what they did here. It is for us, the living, rather to be dedicated here to the unfinished work which they who fought here have thus far so nobly advanced. It is rather for us to be here

dedicated to the great task remaining before us, that from these honored dead we take increased devotion to that cause for which they gave the last full measure of devotion; that we here highly resolve that these dead shall not have died in vain; that this nation, under God, shall have a new birth of freedom; and that government of the people, by the people, for the people, shall not perish from the earth.

It is commonly supposed that Lincoln originated the immortal phrase which closed this address; but did he? Herndon, his law partner, had given Lincoln, several years previously, a copy of Theodore Parker's addresses. Lincoln read and underscored in this book the words "Democracy is direct self-government, over all the people, by all the people, and for all the people." Theodore Parker may have borrowed his phraseology from Webster who had said, four years earlier, in his famous reply to Hayne: "The people's government, made for the people, made by the people, and answerable to the people." Webster may have borrowed his phraseology from President James Monroe who had given voice to the same idea a third of a century earlier. And to whom was James Monroe indebted? Five hundred years before Monroe was born, Wyclif had said, in the preface to the translation of the Scriptures, that "this Bible is for the government of the people, by the people, and for the people." And long before Wyclif lived, more than 400 years before the birth of Christ, Cleon, in an address to the men of Athens, spoke of a ruler "of the people, by the people, and for the people." And from what ancient source Cleon drew his inspiration, is a matter lost in the fog and night of antiquity.

How little there is that is new! How much even the great speakers owe to their reading and to their association with books!

Books! There is the secret! He who would enrich and enlarge his stock of words must soak and tan his mind constantly in the vats of literature. "The only lamentation that I always feel in the presence of a library," said John Bright, "is that life is too short and I have no hope of a full enjoyment of the ample repast spread before me." Bright left school at fifteen, and went to work in a cotton mill, and he never had the chance of schooling again. Yet he became one of the most brilliant speakers of the generation, famous for his superb command of the English language. He read and studied and copied in notebooks and committed to memory long passages from the poetry of Byron and Milton, and Wordsworth and Whittier, and Shakespeare and Shelley. He went through "Paradise Lost" each year to enrich his stock of words.

Charles James Fox read Shakespeare aloud to improve his style. Gladstone called his study a "Temple of Peace," and in it he kept 15,000 books. He was helped most, he confessed, by reading the works of St. Augustine, Bishop Butler, Dante, Aristotle, and Homer. The *Iliad* and the *Odyssey* enthralled him. He wrote six books on Homeric poetry and Homeric times.

The younger Pitt's practice was to look over a page or two of Greek or Latin and then to translate the passage into his own language. He did this daily for ten years, and "he acquired an almost unrivalled power of putting his thoughts, without premeditation, into words well selected and well arranged."

Demosthenes copied Thucydides' history eight times in his own handwriting in order that he might acquire the majestic and impressive phraseology of that famous historian. The result? Two thousand years later, in order to improve his style, Woodrow Wilson studied the works of Demosthenes. Mr. Asquith found his best training in reading the works of Bishop Berkeley.

Tennyson studied the Bible daily. Tolstoy read and reread the Gospels until he knew long passages by memory. Ruskin's mother forced him by steady, daily toil to memorize long chapters of the Bible and to read the entire Book through aloud each year, "every syllable, hard names and all, from Genesis to the Apocalypse." To that discipline and study Ruskin attributed his taste and style in literature.

R. L. S. are said to be the best loved initials in the English language. Robert Louis Stevenson was essentially a writer's writer. How did he develop the charming style that made him famous? Fortunately, he has told us the story himself.

> Whenever I read a book or a passage that particularly pleased me, in which a thing was said or an effect rendered with propriety, in which there was either some conspicuous force or some happy distinction in the style, I must sit down at once and set myself to ape that quality. I was unsuccessful, and I knew it; and tried again, and was again unsuccessful, and always unsuccessful; but at least in these vain bouts I got some practice in rhythm, in harmony, in construction and coordination of parts.
>
> I have thus played the sedulous ape to Hazlitt, to Lamb, to Wordsworth, to Sir Thomas Browne, to Defoe, to Hawthorne, to Montaigne.
>
> That, like it or not, is the way to learn to write; whether I have profited or not, that is the way. It was the way Keats learned, and there never was a finer temperament for literature than Keats'.
>
> It is the great point of these imitations that there still shines beyond the student's reach, his inimitable model. Let him try as he please, he is still sure of failure; and it is an old and very true saying that failure is the only highroad to success.

Enough of names and specific stories. The secret is out. Lincoln wrote it to a young man eager to become a successful lawyer: "It is only to get the books and to read and study them carefully. Work, work, work is the main thing."

What books? Begin with Arnold Bennett's *How to Live on Twenty-four Hours a Day*. This book will be as stimulating as a cold bath. It will tell you a lot about that most interesting of all subjects—yourself. It will reveal to you how much time you are wasting each day, how to stop the wastage, and how to utilize what you salvage. The entire book has only 103 pages. You can get through it easily in a week. Tear out twenty pages each morning, put them in your hip pocket. Then offer up upon the altar of the morning newspaper only ten minutes instead of the customary twenty or thirty minutes.

"I have given up newspapers in exchange for Tacitus and Thucydides, for Newton and Euclid," wrote Thomas Jefferson, "and I find myself much the happier." Don't you believe that you, by following Jefferson's example at least to the extent of cutting your newspaper reading in half, would find yourself happier and wiser as the weeks go by? Aren't you, at any rate, willing to try it for a month, and to devote the time you have thus salvaged to the more enduring value of a good book? Why not read the pages you are to carry with you while waiting for elevators, for buses, for food, for appointments?

After you have read those twenty pages, replace them in the book, tear out another twenty. When you have consumed them all, put a rubber band around the covers to hold the loose pages in place. Isn't it better far to have a book butchered and mutilated in that fashion, with its message in your head, than to have it reposing unbruised and unread upon the shelves of your library?

After you have finished *How to Live on Twenty-four Hours a Day,* you may be interested in another book by the same author. Try *The Human Machine.* This book will enable you to handle people more tactfully. It will develop your poise and self-possession. These books are recommended here not only for what they say, but for the way they say it, for the enriching and refining effect they are sure to have upon your vocabulary.

Some other books that will be helpful are suggested: *The Octopus* and *The Pit,* by Frank Norris, are two of the best American novels ever written. The first deals with turmoils and human tragedies occurring in the wheat fields of California; the second portrays the battles of the bears and bulls on the Chicago Board of Trade. *Tess of the D'Urbervilles,* by Thomas Hardy, is one of the most beautiful tales ever written. *A Man's Value to Society,* by Newell Dwight Hillis and Professor William James' *Talks to Teachers* are two books well worth reading. *Ariel, A Life of Shelley,* by André Maurois, Byron's *Childe Harold's*

Pilgrimage and Robert Louis Stevenson's *Travels with a Donkey* should also be on your list.

Make Ralph Waldo Emerson your daily companion. Command him to give you first his famous essay on "Self-Reliance." Let him whisper into your ear marching sentences like these:

> Speak your latent conviction, and it shall be the universal sense; for always the inmost becomes the outmost,—and our first thought is rendered back to us by the trumpets of the Last Judgment. Familiar as the voice of the mind is to each, the highest merit we ascribe to Moses, Plato, and Milton, is that they set at naught books and traditions, and spoke not what men said but what they thought. A man should learn to detect and watch that gleam of light which flashes across his mind from within, more than the lustre of the firmament of bards and sages. Yet he dismisses without notice his thought, because it is his. In every work of genius we recognize our own rejected thoughts: they come back to us with a certain alienated majesty. Great works of art have no more affecting lesson for us than this. They teach us to abide by our spontaneous impression with good-humoured inflexibility then most when the whole cry of voices is on the other side. Else, to-morrow a stranger will say with masterly good sense precisely what we have thought and felt all the time, and we shall be forced to take with shame our own opinion from another.
>
> There is a time in every man's education when he arrives at the conviction that envy is ignorance; that imitation is suicide; that he must take himself for better, for worse, as his portion; that though the wide universe is full of good, no kernel of nourishing corn can come to him but through his toil bestowed on that plot of ground which is given to him to till. The power which resides in him is new in nature, and none but he knows what that is which he can do, nor does he know until he has tried.

But we have really left the best authors to the last. What

are they? When Sir Henry Irving was asked to furnish a list of what he regarded as the hundred best books, he replied: "Before a hundred books, commend me to the study of two—the Bible and Shakespeare." Sir Henry was right. Drink from these two great fountain sources of English literature. Drink long and often. Toss your evening newspaper aside and say, "Shakespeare, come here and talk to me tonight of Romeo and his Juliet, of Macbeth and his ambition."

If you do these things, what will be your reward? Gradually, unconsciously but inevitably, your diction will begin to take on added beauty and refinement. Gradually, you will begin to reflect somewhat the glory and beauty and majesty of your companions. "Tell me what you read," observed Goethe, "and I will tell you what you are."

This reading program that I have suggested will require little but will power, little but a more careful husbanding of time. . . . You can purchase pocket copies of Emerson's essays and Shakespeare's plays for fifty cents each.

The Secret of Mark Twain's Way with Words

How did Mark Twain develop his delightful facility with words? As a young man, he traveled all the way from Missouri to Nevada by the ponderously slow and really painful stage coach. Food—and sometimes even water—had to be carried for both passengers and horses. Extra weight might have meant the difference between safety and disaster; baggage was charged for by the ounce; and yet Mark Twain carried with him a Webster's Unabridged Dictionary over mountain passes, across scorched deserts, and through a land infested with bandits and Indians. He wanted to make himself master of words, and with his characteristic courage and common sense, he set about doing the things necessary to bring that mastery about.

Both Pitt and Lord Chatham studied the dictionary

twice, every page, every word of it. Browning pored over it daily, finding in it entertainment as well as instruction. Lincoln "would sit in the twilight," records his biographers, Nicolay and Hay, "and read a dictionary as long as he could see." These are not exceptional instances. Every writer and speaker of distinction has done the same.

Woodrow Wilson was superbly skillful with the English language. Some of his writings—parts of his Declaration of War against Germany—will undoubtedly take a place in literature. Here is his own story of how he learned to marshal words:

> My father never allowed any member of his household to use an incorrect expression. Any slip on the part of one of the children was at once corrected; any unfamiliar word was immediately explained; each of us was encouraged to find a use for it in our conversation so as to fix it in our memories.

A New York speaker who is often complimented upon the firm texture of his sentences and the simple beauty of his language, during the course of a conversation recently, lifted the embargo on the secret of his power to choose true and incisive words. Each time he discovers an unfamiliar word in conversation or reading matter, he notes it in his memorandum book. Then, just prior to retiring at night, he consults his dictionary and makes the word his own. If he has gathered no material in this fashion during the day, he studies a page or two of Fernald's *Synonyms, Antonyms and Prepositions,* noting the exact meaning of the words which he would ordinarily interchange as perfect synonyms. A new word a day—that is his motto. This means in the course of a year three hundred and sixty-five additional tools for expression. These new words are stored away in a small pocket notebook, and their meanings reviewed at odd moments during the day. He has found that a word becomes a permanent acquisition to his vocabulary when he has used it three times.

Romantic Stories Behind the Words You Use

Use a dictionary not only to ascertain the meaning of the word, but also to find its derivation. Its history, its origin is usually set down in brackets after the definition. Do not imagine for a moment that the words you speak each day are only dull, listless sounds. They are reeking with color; they are alive with romance. You cannot, for example, say so prosaic a thing as "Telephone the grocer for sugar," without using words that we have borrowed from many different languages and civilizations. *Telephone* is made from two Greek words, *tele,* meaning far, and *phone,* meaning sound. *Grocer* comes from an old French word, *grossier,* and the French came from the Latin, *grossarius;* it literally means one who sells by the wholesale or gross. We got our word *sugar* from the French; the French borrowed it from the Spanish; the Spanish lifted it from the Arabic; the Arabic took it from the Persian; and the Persian word *shaker* was derived from the Sanskrit *carkara,* meaning candy.

You may work for or own a *company. Company* is derived from an old French word meaning *companion;* and *companion* is literally *com,* with, and *panis,* bread. Your *companion* is one with whom you have bread. A *company* is really an association of people who are trying to make their bread together. Your *salary* literally means your *salt* money. The Roman soldiers drew a certain allowance for salt, and one day some wag spoke of his entire income as his *salarium,* and created a bit of slang which has long since become respectable English. You are holding in your hand a *book.* It literally means *beech,* for a long time ago the Anglo-Saxons scratched their words on *beech* trees and on tablets of *beech* wood. The *dollar* that you have in your pocket literally means *valley. Dollars* were first coined in St. Joachim's *Thaler* or *dale* or *valley* in the sixteenth century.

The words *janitor* and *January* have both come down from the name of an Etruscan blacksmith who lived in Rome and made a specialty of locks and bolts for doors.

When he died, he was deified as a pagan god, and was represented as having two faces, so that he could look both ways at the same time, and was associated with the opening and closing of doors. So the month that stood at the close of one year and the opening of another was called *January,* or the month of *Janus.* So when we talk of *January* or a *janitor,* a keeper of doors, we are honoring the name of a blackmsith who lived a thousand years before the birth of Christ and who had a wife by the name of Jane.

The seventh month, *July,* was named after Julius Cæsar; so the Emperor Augustus, not to be outdone, called the next month *August.* But the eighth month had only thirty days at that time, and Augustus did not propose to have the month named after him any shorter than a month named after Julius; so he took one day away from February and added it to August, and the marks of this vainglorious theft are evident on the calendar hanging in your home today. Truly, you will find the history of words fascinating.

Try looking up in a large dictionary the derivation of these words: atlas, boycott, cereal, colossal, concord, curfew, education, finance, lunatic, panic, palace, pecuniary, sandwich, tantalize. Get the stories behind them. It will make them doubly colorful, doubly interesting. You will use them, then, with added zest and pleasure.

Rewriting One Sentence a Hundred and Four Times

Strive to say precisely what you mean, to express the most delicate nuances of thought. That is not always easy—not even for experienced writers. Fanny Hurst told me that she sometimes rewrote her sentences from fifty to a hundred times. Only a few days prior to the conversation she said she had rewritten one sentence one hundred and four times by actual count. Mabel Herbert Urner confided to me that she sometimes spent an entire afternoon eliminating only one or two sentences from a short story that was to be syndicated through the newspapers.

Gouverneur Morris has told how Richard Harding Davis labored incessantly for just the right word:

> Every phrase in his fiction was, of all the myriad phrases he could think of, the fittest in his relentless judgment to survive. Phrases, paragraphs, pages, whole stories even, were written over and over again. He worked upon a principle of elimination. If he wished to describe an automobile turning in at a gate, he made first a long and elaborate description from which there was omitted no detail, which the most observant pair of eyes in Christendom has ever noted with reference to just such a turning. Thereupon he would begin a profess of omitting one by one those details which he had been at such pains to recall; and after each omission he would ask himself, "Does the picture remain?" If it did not he restored the detail which he had just omitted, and experimented with the sacrifice of some other, and so on, and so on, until after Herculean labor there remained for the reader one of those swiftly flashed ice-clear pictures (complete in every detail) with which his tales and romances are so delightfully and continuously adorned.

Most of us have neither time nor disposition to search so diligently for words. These instances are cited to show you the importance successful writers attach to proper diction and expression, in the hope that it may encourage students to take an increased interest in the use of English. It is, of course, not practical for a speaker to hesitate in a sentence and *uh-uh* about, hunting for the word which will exactly express the shade of meaning he desires to convey, but he should practice preciseness of expression in his daily intercourse until it comes unconsciously. He should, but does he? He does not.

Milton is reported to have employed eight thousand words, and Shakespeare fifteen thousand. A Standard Dictionary contains fifty thousand less than half a million; but the average man, according to popular estimates, gets along with approximately two thousand. He has some verbs, enough connectives to stick them together, a handful of nouns, and a few overworked adjectives. He is too lazy, mentally, or too absorbed in business, to train for precision and exactness. The result? Let me give you an illustration. I once spent a few unforgettable days on the rim of the Grand Canyon of the Colorado. In the course of an afternoon, I heard a lady apply the same adjective to a Chow dog, an orchestral selection, a man's disposition, and the Grand Canyon itself. They were all "beautiful."

What should she have said? Here are the synonyms that Roget lists for *beautiful*. Which adjectives do you think she should have employed?

Adjective: *beautiful,* beauteous, handsome, pretty, lovely, graceful, elegant, exquisite, delicate, dainty.

comely, fair, goodly, bonny, good-looking, well-favored, well-formed, well-proportioned, shapely, symmetrical, harmonious.

bright, bright-eyed, rosy-cheeked, rosy, ruddy, blooming, in full bloom.

trim, trig, tidy, neat, spruce, smart, jaunty, dapper.

brilliant, shining, sparkling, radiant, splendid, resplendent, dazzling, glowing, glossy, sleek, rich, gorgeous, superb, magnificent, grand, fine.

artistic, æsthetic, picturesque, pictorial, enchanting, attractive, becoming, ornamental.

perfect, unspotted, spotless, immaculate, undeformed, undefaced.

passable, presentable, tolerable, not amiss.

The synonyms just quoted have been taken from Roget's *Treasury of Words.* It is an abridged edition of Roget's *Thesaurus.* What a help this book is. Personally, I never write without having it at my elbow. I find occasion to use it ten times as often as I use the dictionary.

What years of toil Roget consecrated to its making; yet it will come and sit on your desk and serve you a lifetime for the price of an inexpensive necktie. It is not a book to be stored away on a library shelf. It is a tool to be used constantly. Use it when writing out and polishing the diction of your talks. Use it in dictating your letters and your committee reports. Use it daily, and it will double and treble your power with words.

Shun Worn-Out Phrases

Strive not only to be exact, but to be fresh and original. Have the courage to say the thing as you see it, for "the God of things as they are." For example, shortly after the Flood, some original mind first used the comparison, "cool as a cucumber." It was extraordinarily good then because it was extraordinarily fresh. Even as late as Belshazzar's famous feast, it may still have retained enough of its pristine vigor to warrant its use in an after-dinner speech. But what man who prides himself on his originality would be guilty of repeating it at this somewhat late date?

Here are a dozen similes to express coldness. Aren't they just as effective as the hackneyed "cucumber" comparison, and far fresher and more acceptable?

Cold as a frog.
Cold as a hot-water bag in the morning.
Cold as a ramrod.
Cold as a tomb.
Cold as Greenland's icy mountains.
Cold as clay.—*Coleridge.*
Cold as a turtle.—*Richard Cumberland.*
Cauld as the drifting snow.—*Allan Cunningham.*
Cold as salt.—*James Huneker.*
Cold as an earthworm.—*Maurice Maeterlinck.*
Cold as dawn.
Cold as rain in autumn.

While the mood is upon you, think now of similes of your own to convey the idea of coldness. Have the courage to be distinctive. Write them here:

Cold as....................
Cold as....................
Cold as....................
Cold as....................
Cold as....................

I once asked Kathleen Norris how style could be developed. "By reading classics of prose and poetry," she replied, "and by critically eliminating stock phrases and hackneyed expressions from your work."

A magazine editor once told me that when he found two or three hackneyed expressions in a story submitted for publication, he returned it to the author without wasting time reading it; for, he added, one who has no originality of expression will exhibit little originality of thought.

Summary

1. We have only four contacts with people. We are evaluated and classified by four things: by what we do, by how we look, by what we say, and how we say it. How often we are judged by the language we use. Charles W. Eliot, after he had been president of Harvard for a third of a century, declared: "I recognize but one mental acquisition as a necessary part of the education of a lady or gentleman, namely, an accurate and refined use of the mother tongue."

2. Your diction will be very largely a reflection of the company you keep. So follow Lincoln's example and keep company with the masters of literature. Spend your evenings, as he often did, with Shakespeare and the other great poets and masters of prose. Do that and unconsciously, inevitably, your mind will be enriched and your diction will take on something of the glory of your companions.

3. "I have given up newspapers in exchange for Tacitus and Thucydides, for Newton and Euclid," wrote Thomas Jefferson, "and I find myself much the happier." Why not follow his example? Don't give up the newspapers completely, but skim through in half the time you now devote to them. Give the time you thus salvage to the reading of some enduring book. Tear out twenty or thirty pages from such a volume, carry them in your pocket, read them at odd moments during the day.

4. Read with a dictionary by your side. Look up the unfamiliar word. Try to find a use for it so that you may fix it in your memory.

5. Study the derivation of the words you use. Their histories are not dull and dry; often they are replete with romance. For example, the word *salary* really means *salt*

money. The Roman soldiers were given an allowance for the purchase of salt. Some wag one day created a bit of slang by referring to his wage as his *salt money*.

6. Don't use shopworn, threadbare words. Be precise, exact, in your meaning. Keep Roget's *Treasury of Words* on your desk. Refer to it often. Don't qualify as "beautiful" everything that is appealing to the eye. You may convey your meaning more precisely and with more freshness and beauty if you employ some synonym of *beautiful* —such as *elegant, exquisite, handsome, dainty, shapely, jaunty, dapper, radiant, dazzling, gorgeous, superb, magnificent, picturesque*, etc.

7. Don't use trite comparisons such as "cool as a cucumber." Strive for freshness. Create similes of your own. Have the courage to be distinctive.

APPENDIX

APPENDIX

Speech Building with Exercises

Words Often Mispronounced

Exercise 1

Do you accent the following words on their last syllables? If not, you should do so.

aDEPT
adDICT (verb)
adDRESS
aDULT
conTEST (verb)
deTOUR
disCHARGE
disCOURSE
doMAIN
enCORE
exPERT (adj.)
freQUENT (verb)
griMACE
improVISE
magaZINE
preTENSE
proTEST (verb)
reCOURSE
reSEARCH
reSOURCE
roBUST
roMANCE
rouTINE

Exercise 2

Do you always accent the second syllables of the following words?

abDOmen	inEXplicable
acCLImate	inQUIry
alTERnately	irREVocable
conDOLence	lyCEum
exPOnent	muNICipal
fiNANCE (noun and verb)	muSEum
inCOGnito	orDEal
inCOMparable	SeATtle

The first syllable of *finance*—both verb and noun—may be pronounced *fĭn* (*i* as in *it*), or *fī* (*i* as in *ice*); but remember that the accent must go on the last syllable. This word is commonly mispronounced. Watch it.

The first syllable of *predecessor* may be *prĕd* (*e* as in *met*), or *prē* (*e* as in *eel*); but the third, not the first, syllable must be accented—predeCESSor.

Can you pronounce correctly the italicized words in the following sentences? If in doubt, see Chapter I.

1. In his *address,* the *expert* agriculturist made no *pretense* whatever to having done any original *research.*

2. Do *adults* read the *romances* appearing in the *magazines?*

3. He *protested* that we would not *detour.*

4. He said in a *robust* voice that he would *contest* the decision as a matter of *routine.*

Exercise 3

Do you always accent the following words on their first syllables? This is required for good English.

ADdict (noun)
ADmirable
ADvent
ADverse
AFfluence
Alias
CARton
CHAStisement
COMbat
COMbatant
COMparable
CONcrete (noun and adjective)
CONtrary
CONversant (adjective)
DECade
DEFicit
DESpicable
EXquisite
FORmidable
GONdola
HARass
HOSpitable
IMpotent
INdustry
INterested
INteresting
JUStifiable
LAMentable
MAINtenance
MISchievous
ORdinarily
PACifist
PREamble
PREFerable
PRImarily
RESpite
REVocable
TEMporarily
TRAVerse
THEater
VEhement
VOLuntarily

Can you pronounce correctly the italicized words in these sentences?

1. An *inquiry* was instituted to determine why the *adult* was traveling *incognito.*

2. Each of the *municipal* employees made a *pretense* of having a *robust* pain in his *abdomen.*

3. The *adult* told in his *address* how the *museum* is *financed.*

4. After he becomes *acclimated,* he will be more *robust* physically and more *adept* at his duties.

5. The order for his *discharge* was *irrevocable.*

6. He *financed* the entire *domain.*

7. She went to the *lyceum* in a *gondola* of *incomparable* beauty of lines.

Exercise 4

How many of the following words do you hear mispronounced almost daily? One may say AD-dress for ad-DRESS, and A-dult for a-DULT, and find his errors undetected by many educated people; but who can forgive such slovenly, such gross faults as "praps" and "presidunt" and "progrum"? They are as offensive to the cultivated ear as soiled linen to the eye. For them and their ilk, there can be no excuse, no forgiveness, no explanation except sheer intellectual lethargy and frowziness. Their use condemns one as lacking in culture, as deficient in mental self-respect. Yet I have heard an occasional radio announcer speak of the "progrum." Have you?

Do not say:

except	for accept
agin	" again
ailmunt	" ailment
ambassadur	" ambassador
becuz	" because
unuther	" another
barrul	" barrel
cramberry	" cranberry
crejulus	" credulous
ejucation	" education
fillum	" film
forchin	" fortune
frum	" from
fu-ul	" fuel
genl'mun	" gentlemen
guv'ment	" government
indivijual	" individual
kep'	" kept
lemme	" let me

levul	for level
literachoor	" literature
marvul	" marvel
meludy	" melody
modust	" modest
nearust	" nearest
novus	" novice
parsnup	" parsnip
praps	" perhaps
perul	" peril
pitcher	" picture
poum	" poem
portrut	" portrait
perdicament	" predicament
presidunt	" president
progrum	" program
reco'nize	" recognize
sassy	" saucy
savij	" savage
slep	" slept
spirut	" spirit
stiddy	" steady
supprised	" surprised
swep	" swept
turnup	" turnip
victum	" victim
wuz	" was

Exercise 5

Do you sound the *I's* capitalized in the following, as the "i" in ice? Do it.

bIography	fInis
clIentele	trIbunal
dIgest (noun)	vIand (not veand)

Do you sounds the *I's* and the *Y's* capitalized in the following like the *I* in it? This is the correct sound.

admIrable	genuIne
antI	hemI-
antIdote	hYpocrisy
civilIzation	indIgestion
conspIracy	Italian
cowardIce	Italic
dIgestion	lubrIcate
dIploma	nitro-glycerIne
dIplomacy	semI-
dIvorce	sInce (not sĕns)
FascIstI—(fă-shis-ti)	mischIevous (chĭv-ŭs, not che-vŭs)
fInancial	
fragIle	

The *I* in *mercantile* should be sounded, not as the *e* in *eel,* but as either *i* in *it* or *i* in *ice.*

The *E's* capitalized in the following should be sounded as *e* in *eel.*

abstEmious	pEnalize
amEnable	pEriod
cafetEria (*e* not *a*)	pEriodic
crEdence	sacrilEgious
hystEria	sEnile

Do not say "crik" for "creek"; "klik" for "clique" (klēk); "slik" for "sleek"; nor "soot" for "suite" (swēt).

The *E's* capitalized in the following should be sounded as *e* in *ebb.*

carburEtor	eugEnics
dEaf	tEpid
ephEmeral	

Exercise 6

Do you sound the capitalized *O's* in the following, as *o* in *go?* You should.

HOnOlulu	ZOology
Orient	ZOological

Do you ever hear anyone say *putatuh* and *tubaccuh?* Do you always sound the *O's* in such words as

mosquito	Toronto
piano	widow
pillow	window
tomato	swallow
Toledo	

Do you sound the capitalized *O's* in the following as *o* in *odd?* You should.

catalOg	dOmicile
cOllect	hOrrid
cOlloquial	prOduce (noun)
dOlorous	stOlid

The *O's* capitalized in the following should be sounded, not as *oo* in *book,* but as *oo* in *ooze.*

brOOm	hOOf
cOOp	hOOp
fOOd	nOOn
pOOr	rOOt
rOOf	sOOn
rOOm	spOOn

The *cou* in *coupon* is pronounced *coo*—the *oo* sounded as in *ooze*. Do not say *cuepon.*

Can you pronounce, with sureness and ease, the italicized words in the following? The correct pronunciation of these words has been given in the preceding chapters.

He played an *Italian melody* of *incomparable beauty* with *admirable* and *exquisite* tenderness. *Ordinarily* the old *Lyceum theater* would have been *swept* with applause, and the *President* would have demanded an *encore*. But, this time, *lamentable* to record, some of the *adults* in the audience, troubled with *indigestion,* were suffering from *genuine* pains in the *abdomen;* others were *deaf;* and there was a *clique, interested primarily* in *eugenics,* who declared it was *sacrilegious* to play on Sunday and *contrary* to the ideals of *civilization.* They were not *amenable* to reason; they were bereft of every *fragile* shred of *hospitable diplomacy;* so, in a fit of *hysteria,* they burst into the *Italian's suite* at the hotel, *harassed* the artist, hurled *turnips* and *cranberries* and *nitro-glycerine* at him and *protested* that he must be *penalized* for playing on Sunday. It was a *lamentable* display of *cowardice* and *hypocrisy,* for their *genuine* grievance was not with the day but with the *financial* arrangements *irrevocably* made by their *finance* committee.

Exercise 7

Accent the final *s* sound in the following words:

ships	masts
casks	casts
tasks	mists
masks	fists
nests	posts
guests	roads

How do you pronounce *gasoline* and *Jerusalem?*

Utter the following words in pairs. Make the distinction very plain between the *s* and *z* sounds.

boost—booze	hiss—his
bust—buzz	lace—glazed
cost—because	mace—maize
cease—seize	mess—mezzanine
face—phase	most—mosey
fest—fez	muscle—muzzle
gasoline—gaze	post—pose
gust—guzzle	puss—puzzle
haste—hazed	race—raise

Can you pronounce correctly all the italicized words in the following paragraph? If in doubt, consult the exercises in pronunciation given in the previous lessons.

A seed house in *Honolulu* sent its *catalog* to the *address* of a certain *adult* whose *domicile* was on the banks of a *creek* near the *Zoological* gardens in *Toledo.*

This poor fellow was a drug *addict*. When he was under the influence of opium, he *marveled* at the *surprisingly* beautiful *pictures* of *tomatoes* and *parsnips* and melons in the sales *literature*. He dreamed dreams. . . . In spite of the fact that he was a *poor* man, and, at times, found it difficult to keep a *roof* over his head, nevertheless, he now ordered *surprisingly* large quantities of seeds, far larger quantities than were *justifiable,* considering his *finances.* For some *inexplicable* reason, the *credulous* chap felt that he could make a *fortune* raising *produce;* so, in order to collect cash, he *voluntarily* sold his *piano,* his *spoons,* his cigar store *coupons,* the *carburetor* of his Ford, the *broom* that *swept* his *rooms* and even the very *food* in his *domicile.* He wrote the *Honolulu* concern, saying: "*Gentlemen,* I am very much *interested* in your *admirable catalog* showing the *exquisite* profits to be made in the truck raising *industry.* I am an *Italian* and belong to the *Fascisti.* I knife the *Bolsheviki.* I have a *diploma.* At times, I also have a pain in the *abdomen* due to *indigestion,* but as *soon* as I put a flower on my coat, the *mischievous* hurt becomes *impotent.* I can sell to a *cafeteria* here all the *produce* I raise, so please send me at once a *barrel* of *tomato* and *turnip* and *parsnip* seeds, and the *roots* of a *cranberry* bush." . . . Thus ends the *rocking* and *shocking romance. Finis.*

Exercise 8

The *A's* which are capitalized in the following should be sounded as "a" in *day:*

alma mAter
Apex
apparAtus
Aviation
Aviator
blAtant
cadAver
dAta
grAtis
ignorAmus
implAcable
LusitAnia
(sound all *I's* as in *it.*)
prefAce
pro rAta
quAsi
rAdiator
sAlient
stAtus
strAta
tornAdo
ultimAtum
utilitArian
verbAtim

Can you pronounce correctly all the italicized words in the following story?

Once upon a time, a *stolid* and *senile* Prince of the *Orient* read a *poem* about love. With the *advent* of spring, a hunger for *romance* stole over him, and he was unable to *combat* it. It was so *exquisite,* so *formidable,* so *inexplicable,* so *delicious,* so *dolorous,* so *shaking* and *quaking,* that he did not even desire to *combat* it. He felt that no one in the wide *domains* of his native land could understand the *marvelous melody* that *swept* through his heart. Consequently, he began to *frequent* the harbor, watching the stately *ships* sail in with high *masts* through the *mists.* His *finances* hardly permitted travel; so he went about *incognito,* using an *alias,* while he sold *alternately brooms* and cigar store *coupons* until he was able to stand the *financial* strain of a trip to *Seattle.* There he met a *fragile widow,* who had also recently *divorced* a drug *addict.* Although he was not *conversant* with her language, he was an *expert* flatterer. However, she was *tepid* to his advances. She counted the *cost because* she did not want to marry in *haste* when her own mind was *hazy.* She *hissed* in his *face* that she was not *interested* in his proposal, that marriage with him would be *horrid, despicable, contrary* to her ideals. He received his *chastisement* in silence, tore up the *trousseau* that he had depleted his *finances* to purchase, and, *moaning* and *groaning,* he sailed back to *Honolulu.*

Exercise 9

Do you sound the *A's* capitalized in the following as the *a* in *arm?*

Aunt
drAma
heArth

Do you sound all the *A's* capitalized in the following words as you sound the *a* in *soda* and *sofa,* and as you should sound the *a* in *ask?* Few do. This first shade-vowel sound of *a* is difficult to describe on paper. It is not the *a* in *hat;* neither is it the *a* in *arm.* It is between them. However, if one must err, it had better be in under-doing rather than in over-doing it. At all hazards, avoid anything that smacks of affectation. Isn't it far better, at least in the United States, to mispronounce the *a* in *bath* and *half,* giving it the sound of *a* in *cat,* rather than to go to the other extreme and use the sound of *a* as in *arm?*

advAnce	cAlf
advAntage	cAn't
Afternoon	cAsh
Answer	cAsket
Ask	cAst
bAsket	clAsp
bAss (fish)	contrAst
bAth	dAnce
behAlf	demAnd
blAst	drAft
brAnch	fAst
brAss	flAsk

gAsp	lAugh
ghAstly	mAster
girAffe	pAss
glAnce	pAst
glAss	pAstor
grAft	pAth
grAnt	plAnt
grAsp	repAst
grAss	shAft
hAlf	shAn't (slang)
lAss	slAnt
lAst	tAsk

Exercise 10

The *o* in *comely,* and the capitalized *U's* in *sUpple, sUburban* and *lUscious* are sounded as *u* in *up.*

The letters capitalized in the following should be sounded, not as the *oo* in *ooze,* but as the *u* in *futility* and *music.* This, the long *U* sound, consists of a close union of the sound of *i* in *it,* and the *oo* in *ooze.* The precise sounding of the long *u* is rare and is an infallible sign of cultured pronunciation. In a few words, it is always enunciated correctly. For example, we never say *moosic* for *music, foo* for *few, food* for *feud, footure* for *future, boogle* for *bugle,* or *coopid* for *cupid;* but how many of us say *noo* for *new, dooty* for *duty,* and *Toosday* for *Tuesday!*

absolUte
assUme
attitUde
avenUe
carbUretor
constitUtion
consUme
credUlity
cUlinary
delUde
delUsion
dEW
dilUte
dUbious
dUe
dUet
dUke
dUly
dUty
furnitUre
gratitUde
illUsion
institUte
institUtion
lUbricate
LUcy
lUre
lUte
measUre
multitUde
neUtral
nEW

nEWs
nEWspaper
nUcleus
nUde
nUisance
nUmerous
nUtrition
obtUse
opportUnity
pictUre
prodUce
renEW
resolUtion
seclUde
solUtion
stUdent
stUpid
subdUe
sUit
sUpine
tUbe
tUbercUlosis
TUesday
tUmor
tUmult
tUne
tUtor

Exercise 11

These words have four—not three—syllables. Read them aloud correctly.

ac-cu-ra-cy	in-er-ti-a
a-e-ri-al	mem-o-ra-ble
a-mi-a-ble	mis-er-a-ble
a-wak-en-ing	Na-po-le-on
cer-e-mon-y	pneu-mo-ni-a
de-lir-i-ous	pre-pos-ter-ous
de-lir-i-um	ri-dic-u-lous
de-liv-er-y	tem-per-a-ment
dis-cov-er-y	tem-pes-tu-ous
ex-pe-di-ent	u-su-al-ly
gen-er-al-ly	val-u-a-ble
ge-og-ra-phy	ven-er-a-ble
hy-gi-en-ic	

These words have five—not four—syllables.

ac-com-pa-ni-ment
con-sid-er-a-ble
lab-o-ra-to-ry

The words *ath-lete* and *al-ien* have two—not three—syllables. These words have three—not two syllables:

ac-cu-rate	boun-da-ry
bar-ri-er	bur-i-al
bev-er-age	cas-u-al
bois-ter-ous	Cath-o-lic

cel-er-y
ce-re-al
Ches-a-peake
choc-o-late
dex-ter-ous
di-a-mond
em-per-or
fam-i-ly
fed-er-al
fo-li-age
gal-ler-y
gen-er-al
gen-tle-men
gro-cer-y
his-tor-y
i-vo-ry
jo-vi-al
la-bor-er
Laz-a-rus
li-bra-ry
lit-er-al
me-di-um
mem-o-ry

Exercise 12

Do not drop the *H* sound in words like the following. In these the W is pronounced as if it were after the *H;* as *hwy* for *why*. Say:

whack	not wack
wharf	not warf
wheat	not weat
wheel	not weel
when	not wen
whether	not wether
which	not wich
whip	not wip
whiskey	not wiskey
white	not wite
whittle	not wittle
whoa	not wo

Exercise 13

Watch your first syllables: do not substitute *uh* for *a*. Do not say:

uhbate	for abate
uhbout	" about
uhcount	" account
uhdorn	" adorn
uhdress	" address
uhfect	" affect
uhgree	" agree
uhgrieve	" aggrieve
uhlert	" alert
uhlow	" allow
uhmonia	" ammonia
uhnoy	" annoy
uhpear	" appear
uhrest	" arrest
uhsume	" assume
uhtach	" attach

Do not shorten or change the sound of *be* and *de* in the following words. Do not say:

buh-cause	or b'cuz	for because
buh-lieve	" b'lieve	" believe
buh-come	" b'come	" become
buh-fore	" b'fore	" before

buh-gin	or b'gin	for begin
duh-bate	" d'bate	" debate
duh-cide	" d'cide	" decide
duh-test	" d'test	" detest
duh-fer	" d'fer	" defer
duh-gree	" d'gree	" degree

Exercise 14

See if you can pronounce all of the italicized words in the following selection:

On his *awakening,* after the *tempestuous* day, the *aviator* rose from his bed before the broken *hearth* and looked over his *radiator* and *carburetor* carefully to see that they were not injured. After all parts were *lubricated,* even before the *dew* was off the *grass,* he flew *due* east as his *duty* called.

His *aerial* trip was aided by his knowledge of the *geography* of the country. He was an *athlete;* the *boisterous* and *jovial* events of the past evening did not *affect* his *dexterous handling* of the *white* ship. He did not need the *whip* of *whiskey* to *steady* his hand on the *wheel.* Neither did the *memories* of the plaudits of the *gallery* nor the past *history* of his comrades of the squadron *abate* his constant watch over the *boundaries.*